1

Never Give Up

A Developmental Manual for African American Men

K. Tutashinda

This book is intended as a reference volume only, not as a medical, psychiatric, or holistic manual. The information given here is designed to help you make good, informed decisions about your health and wellness. It is not intended as a substitute for any treatment that may have been prescribed by your doctor or holistic practitioner. If you suspect that you have a medical, psychiatric or functional health problem, seek competent help from your Physician, Psychiatrist, or Chiropractor.

Dedication

To my father,
Joe Porche' Altheimer,
Who more than anyone I know,
Embodies the idea, "Never Give Up"

Other Works By K. Tutashinda

Toward a Holistic Worldview: Essays on Control, Technology, and Personal/Social Transformation

Therapeutic Exercises for the Spine

It's Our Time: Ella Baker, Participatory Democracy, and Oakland, California

The Singularity is Already Here: An Indigenous and Grassroots Perspective on Our Technological Future

Whose Future Is It? Social Control and the Health of African American Boys and Men

Nanotechnology, Indigenous Wisdom, and Health: Selected Essays

Political Consciousness as a Prerequisite Vol: 1: On African American Manhood, Race, and Legal History

Contents

8

Preface

In 1979, I read *Mastery Through Accomplishment* by Murshid Hazrat Inayat Khan. In its pages, Murshid mapped out a methodology and path of inward development that incorporated material accomplishments along side spiritual attainment. He felt that attachment to the material world was too much to ask someone to forgo in favor of an exclusively spiritual life. Therefore, in true Sufi fashion, he designed a path whereby an individual could achieve some earthy satisfaction and achievement in order to lessen material attachment.

While this book is not written by a spiritual master, it is inspired by Murshid's insistence that it is absolutely possible to fulfill one's responsibilities as a human, father, husband, son, brother, cousin, uncle, friend, student, comrade, teacher-and remain spiritually focused and committed. To the best of my ability, I attempt to outline some of the inner attributes it takes to, "never give up," in that quest. It is not easy. The tremendous social/political factors stacked against African American men and women are great. We feel them collectively and personally. And there is no getting around the weight of responsibility that we have as a people to provide a structure and platform for future generations to thrive. So far, we have failed to do that.

But that still does not address one's personal dilemma. That is still on us individually. How do we contribute to both our personal development and prosperity and our people's full liberation at the same time? Are they compatible? Do we have to follow a major world religion to have a good life? There are so many questions and few answers. In this book, I try to address some of those questions and identify inner qualities needed to persevere through tumultuous times and personal crises.

These essays, with review questions, exercises, and film suggestions are designed to stimulate thinking and discussion among African American men and women about their individual and collective internal development. The two are irrevocably linked. Despite the tremendous odds stacked against us, we are not victims. When the smoke clears and the fog recedes, we see clearly that as a people we have been sustained, energized, and led by a force that says, "never give up."

Introduction: How To Use This Book

This book is meant to be used as both a self-help manual and as a text for manhood development classes. As a self-help manual, it is designed to stimulate reflection and action around some of the internal attributes needed to be an empowered African American man. As a class or workshop manual, it is meant to be an interactive and experiential workbook. After each essay, there are review questions, classroom exercises, writing assignments, and films chosen specifically to highlight ideas presented in the essay. The idea is to fully immerse the participant in the emotional experience of an idea as much as possible to anchor it physically, somatically.

For example, in discussing intuition, the phrase, 'gut feeling,' is often used. In the context of this manual, the participant would be asked questions exploring the use of 'guts' in popular and folk culture, and to reflect on the actual experience of sensations and tingling in the abdomen or stomach area whenever 'one has a strong feeling about something' or a hunch. Similarly, one gets 'butterflies' in the stomach when one is a bit nervous or apprehensive. Understanding some of the physical manifestations of emotions and ideas is somatics, and this book seeks to make subtle philosophical concepts more tangible by encouraging participants to experience the ideas 'in their bodies.'

Additionally, participants are asked to write several five paragraph long papers on subjects discussed in the accompanying essays. Two appendices, one on note taking, and another on writing a five paragraph paper are included and are designed to help a student reading the book, or an instructor or workshop leader. The idea is that writing is a very important skill and any class on African American manhood development should also incorporate basic academic skill enhancement. **(1)**

While this book seeks to be holistic, it is not comprehensive. There are many areas of African American manhood development that are not discussed. What is discussed are core concepts that have been time tested to help individuals persevere through difficult times. And, given some of the predictions of scientists regarding climate change, unending wars in the Middle East, turmoil on the streets of America, and one's own personal dilemmas, there will be some difficult days ahead. But this is how life is. It is full of challenges. Like the millions who have come before us, we must do all we can to fortify ourselves internally and strengthen ourselves physically to survive, thrive, and prosper. And then, we must find a way to participate, in our own way, in our struggle for equity, justice, and empowerment.

Chapter 1

"Never Give Up:" The Development of an African American Man with Fortitude, Commitment, and A Sense of Responsibility

Abstract

This essay focuses on the creation of an African American Man that is developed internally to withstand the multitude of pressures, stressful situations, and unforeseen circumstances that may arise within his life. Recognizing and understanding that African American men have the shortest life expectancies, highest death rates from homicide, cardiovascular disease, and cancer, as well as have the highest rates of incarceration, unemployment, and drug usage often times complicated by mental illness, this is no small feat. Clearly identifying and outlining specific principles and creating environments and learning situations that inculcate and develop those principles can establish a holistic foundation and mental/emotional attitude that never gives up.

Introduction

More than Anything, It's An Attitude

Because of the crisis faced by African American boys and men, there has been a tremendous response creating books, films, initiatives, and manhood training programs. This outpouring and productivity has been produced by well trained, innovative, and in many cases, brilliant individuals. What would additionally help this work is to focus on some of the internal attributes needed to fully develop and thrive as an African American man. What does a fully developed African American man look like? How does he function, what does he believe, how does he think, and how does he respond to crises? These are some of the questions that need to be asked.

Difficult as it may be, they can be answered with one phrase: he is a man who, never gives up. His Holiness the XIVth Dalai Lama, who leads the refugee community of Tibetan Buddhists, headquartered in Dharamsala, Himachal Pradesh, India said in a talk,

"Never Give Up"

"No Matter what is going on
Never Give Up

Develop the heart
Too much energy in your country
Is spent developing the mind
Instead of the heart
Develop the heart

Be compassionate
Not just to your friends but to everyone
Be compassionate

Work for peace
In your heart and in the world
Work for peace

And I say it again

Never give up
No matter what is happening
No matter what is going on around you

Never give up " (1)

These are the words of a present day spiritual master, but they easily could have been uttered by our African American slave ancestors, or our Native American neighbors, or the countless poor people who have toiled in the fields, factories, and industries of America. Harriet Tubman, Sojourner Truth, Frederick Douglass or Paul Robeson as well as our grandmothers, grandfathers, parents, uncles, and aunts could have spoken these words. The Dalai Lama's message of "Never Give Up" represents the timeless wisdom of intestinal fortitude that has sustained African American and other oppressed communities since the birth of this nation and nothing expresses the attitude of a fully developed African American man better than this phrase.

What set of qualities develops this kind of attitude? What kind of specific training does it require? These are difficult questions and there are no easy answers. All we can do is dig into our collective memory, spiritual and scientific archives, and personal experiences in an attempt to understand some of the essentials to personal success and the development of an attitude that is adaptable, creative, and resilient. In some cases, individuals are emotionally fragile, mentally unbalanced and have difficulties. In those situations, we should not blame the victim, as there may be genetic, family, and social factors at work that could make the task seem insurmountable. And as Michelle Alexander explains in *The New Jim Crow: Mass Incarceration in the Age of Colorblindness* and in *Whose Future is It? Social Control and the Health of African American Boys and Men,* as well as books by Haki Madhubuti, Sidney M. Willhelm, Angela Y. Davis, Dylan Rodriguez, and Loic Wacquant, and others, there is a political and economic advantage in perpetrating a "war on drugs" that equates to a war on the African American and other oppressed communities. This results in, among other realities, a disproportionate number of young men in prison. Yet, at the end of the day, each person must take responsibility for him or herself and try to do the things that are needed to have a productive and meaningful life. No teacher, mentor, manhood development class, or organization by themselves or itself can do it for them. Each person has to dig deep within, like Malcolm X starting with the dictionary and the word aardvark, and transform their own life. No one said it was going to be easy. It is not.

One exceptional and hardworking thinker and teacher amongst us is Haki Madhubuti. He has been working tirelessly for four decades to address some of the problems plaguing our communities. Haki Madhubuti, who along with his wife, Safisha, has created four independent schools, a publishing company, raised four adult children and has written over 31 books consisting of poetry, essays on African American culture, and the present-day and future survival of African American people. Several of his books specifically address issues affecting African American boys and men.

In *Tough Notes: A Healing Call for Creating Exceptional Black Men, Affirmations, Meditations, Readings and Strategies,*

Madhubuti outlines a method for developing exceptional African American men. Though the task is huge and difficult, and even Madhubuti would admit, impossible to systematically program, his suggestions convey the time tested, concrete, practical ideas born out of personal experience. He is writing about something he has done and knows, not something he thinks, researched at a major university, or projected could happen. His chapters on "Empowering the Self," "Finding the Exceptional You," "Women," "Progressive Nurturing: The Saving Grace," and "Liberation," are instructive in that they elucidate for the reader that material wealth, fame, or even power are not the only attributes of an exceptional African American man. **(2)** Exceptional African American men may or may not possess these qualities, but ultimate success, according to Madhubuti, is determined by a set of criteria that encompasses the whole person and includes their commitment to African American liberation and freedom in the fullest sense.

Madhubuti's riveting autobiography, ***YellowBlack: The First Twenty-One Years of a Poet's Life, A Memoir***, illustrates the idea of never giving up. Here, he explains how he personally had to fend for himself and younger sister after his mother died from alcoholism and drug addiction during his early adolescence. In the Prologue poem titled, "Yes," he writes,

"I have nothing of my mother's
but memories
I have no piece of cloth,
Nor any re-read books,
No recipes for spaghetti,
cakes or coleslaw.

There are no photographs of the two of us
Laughing or holding hands,
I don't even remember the beauty of her voice.
All I have deep inside of me are her last
Words, "you are smarter than us Don,
Use the library, take care of your
Sister and learn from what I have done wrong."" **(3)**

Both of these informative books serve as practical manuals on how a young man might extricate himself from a vicious web of low self-esteem, lack of self-knowledge, and poverty to become productive, creative, and empowered. They both clearly explain how and why Madhubuti never gave up.

Equally inspiring is the story of Eboni Boykin. Although this present book focuses more on African American boys and men, it could easily be about African American girls and women. Eboni's story encompasses what both groups and other poor and disadvantaged children face daily in America, homelessness. She was featured on Melissa Harris-Perry's show on MSNBC, as well in an article written by Terrell Jermaine Starr. Starr writes,

"Eboni Boykin spent most of her childhood moving from one homeless shelter to another with her mother in the St. Louis area. She also enrolled in more than 14 schools for one reason or another. But that did not stop her from realizing her dream of being accepted into an Ivy League school, the St. Louis Post-Dispatch reports. The 17-year old senior at Normandy High School has been accepted into Columbia University in New York City on a full scholarship."

Now a junior, Ms. Boykin expressed the tenacity and drive it took for her to achieve her goal with poise and clarity. She said,

"Seeing the absolute worst of life is the ultimate motivation,"

And,

"Getting into Columbia definitely teaches me that just keeping the faith and not giving up pays off. And it just teaches me if you hang in there you can have anything you want if you are willing to work hard for it." **(4)**

While it is obvious that both Haki Madhubuti and Eboni Boykin have achieved seemingly exceptional goals, they have something inside of them that told them to "never give up." They and others who have survived, thrived, and empowered themselves have an inner voice that says, "don't quit." Where does that voice originate, and what qualities must one have to hear those words? And, although everyone potentially has those attributes, how does one tap into them if they are not readily manifested in their lives?

In his autobiography, ***The Window 2 My Soul: My Transformation From A Zone 8 Thug to a Father & Freedom Fighter***, former gang-banger Yusef Shakur outlines how he was able to transform himself-in prison. There, he got to know his father, and because of the tremendous amount of work his father had done on himself, he was able to help his son grow and develop. They both exhibit the "never give up" attitude with great determination. Yusef writes about his transformation:

19

"For seven years, my thinking, values, morals, and behavior would be heavily influenced and dictated by thought patterns that revolved around Black self-hatred; I had internalized these negative thoughts and, ultimately, I released them upon whomever I considered my enemies-through vicious acts of violence. By openly/completely immersing myself in the genocidal-soldier mentality on the streets of Detroit's west side, the notorious "Gang Squad" made it their business to get me off the streets at any cost, even if it meant charging me with a crime I did not commit. ......My prison experience was not your every-day prison experience. While there, I met my father- the man whom I only knew through images. My father immediately began to nurture, teach, and cultivate me into being a responsible and educated black man by being a Beautiful Example of What a Black Man Should Be!" **(5)**

Yusef has since written two more books, speaks nationally, produced a documentary film, started a non-profit and became a full-time college student. His extraordinary story shows how possibilities emerge if one dedicates one's mind to self-growth. What he, Eboni and Haki share is an attitude that never gives up. What supports and assists that attitude, even though they represent three different generations and eras and have different skills, pursuits, and life experiences, is that they all shared an early life of poverty that forged an inner determination grounded in fortitude, commitment, and a sense of responsibility. An investigation of these precepts might be instructive in understanding the philosophical architecture and scaffolding of the "never give up" attitude.

Fortitude

Fortitude is key when it comes to never giving up. It comes from the Latin word, fortitudo, which means *"bravery, strength."* The root word is fortis or *"bravery, strong."* It means *"mental or emotional strength that enables courage in the face of adversity."* **(6)** We should never forget that our slave ancestors had tremendous fortitude. They endured the brutal inhumanity of being captured in Africa, having to march sometimes hundreds of miles to the coast and being held in damp, dark, slave dungeons, and then herded like cattle onto crowded, disease ridden slave ships to the new world. Then, they were broken and beaten and worked like beasts of burden on New World plantations. The amount of strength and will needed to survive this is not to be underestimated. African American young men need the ability to go through life with an understanding that life has ups and downs, and that adversity can make a person stronger. Living in America, at times under extremely adverse conditions and social situations filled with violence, unemployment, incarceration, illness, and death, young and old African American men and women, as well as other poor and disadvantaged people, have to help keep each other strong. Reminding us that our ancestors had fortitude can be useful in instilling it in our young African American men and women.

Often, while rightly celebrating our ancestors who mutinied or revolted, we neglect to praise and affirm the tremendous debt we owe our ancestors who endured, survived, and in some cases, managed to thrive under some of the most inhumane conditions in the history of humankind. They had fortitude. They never gave up. In the context of African American

21

manhood development, and especially in a classroom or workshop setting, this history is pertinent. Photographs, documentary and dramatic film representations, as well as readings, including slave narratives, (with later audio recordings) could serve as powerful tools to create a somatic experience whereby young men and women could viscerally and palpably learn and feel what it took to survive. By re-creating these experiences, memory is instilled that can serve as fuel to ignite and sustain fortitude. Just as a hot air balloon needs a constant source of helium, fortitude needs a constant source of energy. Remembering the struggles of not just slavery, but the African American struggle and the struggles of our families, in general, serve as consistent reminders of how important it is to maintain, and maintain at a high level.

An important aid in teaching fortitude is physical discipline, particularly martial arts training. Martial arts training is more than just learning how to fight or defend oneself. It is about learning how 'not to fight' and have self-control. The intricate techniques of various martial arts styles involve learning history, geography and the unique origins of the particular art form, strategy and the psychology of combat, as well as healing techniques to rejuvenate the body after battle. The comprehensive, whole body learning aspect of martial arts training shows the student in real concrete ways how to persevere through pain and adversity. When an instructor commands the students to do 500 or 1000 punches or kicks despite being tired or exhausted, it pushes them to their physical, mental, and emotional limits. It allows students to see for themselves that there are really no limits to what they can do or at least, their capacity far exceeds their perceived limitations. That is fortitude. It teaches them to "never give up." They realize that they can overcome their limitations because the limitations are in their minds and often time have been put there by society, family members or even teachers. They learn fortitude in a practical way.

There are numerous ways to teach fortitude. The main idea is that each lesson should stress the whole-body learning concept through an experiential exercise. Lecturing about fortitude is instructional, but it does not anchor the idea firmly into the life experiences of the student. The lessons that are most remembered and retained for life, mimic real life experiences and involve the entire body. In this way, there are physical and somatic triggers that are embedded to remind the student physically, emotionally, and intellectually, about the holistic meaning of fortitude. It is similar to how if one experiences a bad or traumatic experience doing a particular activity or at a particular place, each time the person revisits that activity or site, they emotionally re-experience aspects of the traumatic event as if it happened anew. Likewise, it can happen with positive experiences too, especially if they are fully integrated into bodily exercises. Thus, fortitude can be taught such that it is never forgotten.

Commitment

Commitment means, "*the committing of oneself, pledge, promise,*" and "*an obligation, an engagement.*" It originates from the Latin root for commit which is, 'commiterre,' "*to unite, connect, combine; to bring together.*" It is formed by combining com, or "*together,*" + mittere or "*to put, send.*" (**7**) Hence, by definition, commitment involves both a pledge to oneself and the bringing together of others. It is the act of dedicating oneself to following through on what one says they are going to do. It has the same root as community, which inherently implies togetherness. Therefore, in developing an attitude that never gives up, making a commitment to "never give up" is an important pledge to oneself, family and community at the same time. If the individual commits to never giving up, in their quest to better themselves, makes a positive contribution, and strives for the very best in life, even if their commitment is solely in self-interest, both their family and community benefit. This individual commitment means that there is one less person the parents have to support, feed, clothe, and worry about. If they can take care of and support themselves and not infringe upon others, there is one less person disrupting the safety and wellbeing of the community. All of this from a commitment to oneself-if the individual expands their commitment to improve their family's situation and to help their communities in practical, hands-on, tangible ways, everyone benefits. Everyone benefits from individuals making a pledge and commitment to oneself and others to "never give up."

Making a commitment takes discipline to not go back on a pledge. It takes will power and the above-mentioned fortitude to keep the commitment despite adversity, setbacks, and temporary failures. It takes a deep-rooted desire to grow as a person and man or woman and to sincerely care for others. If it is said publically or voiced to others, it makes the commitment public and the community can help hold the individual accountable. In this context, manhood training and rites of passage programs serve as part of the public memory of one's commitment. People can remind one, "but you said…" and the individual is reminded of the commitment as a pact or trust made and meant to be kept. A public declaration of commitment also has the added effect of prompting one to never give up and binds the community together, particularly if other members have made similar commitments. In this way, one person's commitment could spread like wildfire and become contagious.

Commitment is the bedrock of relationships whether it involves being a child, parent, sibling, marriage partner, friend, or comrade in struggle. If one is able to make a commitment, they can commit themselves to never giving up on themselves and others.

Responsibility

Responsibility comes from the French word, *responsible* and Latin word *respondere,* which means, "*to respond.*" It means, "*answerable (to another, for something)*," and "*morally accountable for one's actions.*" **(8)** In a community where more than half of our children are raised in single parent homes, almost as many of our young men are in prison as are in college, and young African American men's chances of being murdered are fifteen times greater than a young white man's, responsibility is a principle and idea of paramount importance. **(9)** Notwithstanding the incredible social forces of capitalist control and political oppression faced by African American people, in general, and men, in particular, many of the serious issues facing us could be tempered by us, particularly African American men, by taking more responsibility. It is not just an issue of jobs, economics, and money, although these are very vital and important issues. The issue of responsibility is about consciousness. We are talking about **Black Consciousness, Political, Global, and Environmental Consciousness, Spiritual Consciousness, and**

Consciousness around all of our responsibilities. In the context of never giving up, having a sense of responsibility is responding to and caring for others with commitment and fortitude. They all come together in responsibility because by definition it involves others, even though one must be responsible for oneself. What African American people need are its men to act responsibly and take responsibilities seriously. Many do, yet there are enough that are absent, unaccountable, and not responsible to their children, parents, siblings, and community such that there is a crisis. Therefore, any African American manhood development class or workshop that exists has to discuss the issue of responsibility.

In terms of African American history and struggle, Frederick Douglass took responsibility for his brethren by speaking out against the injustices of slavery and women's oppression. When Harriet Tubman risked her life by going back into the South to rescue slaves over one hundred times, she was taking responsibility. Part of taking and having a sense of responsibility is the "taking on the burdens of others." **(10)** Those who can are obliged to make the burden of those who are younger, weaker, or infirm, lighter and easier to carry. It is their responsibility. Responsibility is caring. When the young people in the Black Power/Liberation and Black Arts movements gave up money, careers, and material comforts, risking their lives by standing up to the most powerful and violent nation in the history of humankind, they took responsibility. They did not do that just for themselves, as many were college educated and could have easily taken cushy jobs and kept their mouths shut. They chose not to do that. Some of them gave up their lives; some have been in prison for over fifty years. Many are sick and debilitated today without health insurance or 401k retirement pensions. All of their political activism was done because they took responsibility for their entire people and made tremendous sacrifices. Therefore, everyone today, particularly African American men, has to step up and do his part.

Conclusion

These precepts are examples of the characteristics needed to build the foundation for an attitude that never gives up. A never give up attitude is essential in developing will power and will power is necessary in developing mastery. The great Sufi sage, Hazrat Inayat Khan, who is credited with bringing Sufism to America, spoke a great deal about mastery through accomplishment. **(11)** He taught that accomplishing one's goals weakens material attachments and sets the stage for spiritual mastery. The ultimate goal is self-mastery. In the process, he believed that serving humanity, finding and achieving one's purpose of life, and conquering fear and failure were worthy goals. Integral to these, is an attitude of never giving up.

African American men and women have to continue to cultivate this attitude and create new teaching technologies that assist in this process. This is vital to the survival and development of African American people. Our ability to exhibit fortitude, commitment and a sense of responsibility are vital in training African American boys to become men. But, it must be done by example. They must see the principles that are being discussed enacted in real time and within real people. Theoretical constructs and non-experiential philosophy can be helpful, but they are not essential. What is essential are practical lessons that can make philosophical principles tangible. Life lessons need to be easy to comprehend, fun to enact, and involve the whole body such that memory and retention are enhanced. Never giving up is essential. African American men and women are essential and fortitude, commitment, and a sense of responsibility are essential.

Review Questions

1. What does "Never Give Up" mean to you? Can you think of situations where you never gave up? How did you feel? Are there any instances where you gave up and did not finish or complete something important? How did that make you feel? Did anyone ask you why you gave up in that particular instance?

2. What is "Personal power?" How does "Never Give Up" relate to "Personal Power?" Do we gain or lose "Personal Power" by giving up?

3. What does fortitude mean to you? Can you describe some instances where you exhibited fortitude? Can you describe some instances where members of your family exhibited fortitude?

4. What does commitment mean to you? Can you describe some instances where you have exhibited commitment? How did that make you feel? What about family members?

5. What does responsibility mean to you? Can you describe some instances where you exhibited responsibility? How did that make you feel? Have you at one time or another been irresponsible? Did it feel different than being responsible? In what way did it feel different? Can you think of instances where your friends have been irresponsible? What were the consequences?

6. What other ideas or qualities do you think comprise the "Never Give Up" attitude? Is it something that can be immediately learned and put into practice or does it take a long time? How long?

7. Think about this scenario. An African American man is unemployed, but actively looking for a job, married, with four children. He and his wife, who is working, get into continuous arguments, mostly about the fact that he is not working. After years of the situation remaining 'off and on' the same, the man leaves his family and moves in with his parents. He feels that the "system" is unfair, racist, and unjust and that is why he cannot find a job. His wife feels he is lazy, lacks initiative, and has given up on her and their family. Who is right? The husband? The wife? Are they both correct? What do you think the children think and feel in this situation? How does this impact his parents? What if the situation is complicated by the fact that the husband/father is a felon and has served four years in prison prior to getting married and starting a family? Has the husband/father given up? Is he showing fortitude, commitment, and responsibility? How much of this situation is his fault, 50%, 100%, somewhere in between? How much of this situation is society's fault, 50%, 100%, somewhere in between? Is the wife at fault here? His parents? Who suffers the most in this situation, the husband, wife, children, or parents? Does the larger society suffer? Are there any solutions to this situation if he is unable to find a job? If he finds a job, are his problems solved?

8. Think about your life and present situation. Are there any areas of your life where you could use more fortitude, commitment, and sense of responsibility? Are there any areas of your life where you could use more of a "Never Give Up" attitude? Write down those areas and describe how those particular situations would be different if you implemented those qualities. What kind of support

structures around you do you need to implement fortitude, commitment, responsibility, and a never give up attitude in your life? How soon can you begin to implement these qualities or characteristics? What are some of the obstacles preventing you from implementing them immediately? How can those obstacles be removed?

Somatic Exercise-Fortitude

Begin with pushups. Instruct the students by example on how to properly do a pushup. Discuss the specific muscles involved: the triceps in the arms, the pectoralis major in the chest, the abdominals in the stomach region with secondary support by all the muscles of the back and legs, including, multifidi, gluteals, hamstrings, and gastrocnemius in the legs. In this way, the students learn experiential anatomy and somatics while doing the exercise. Start with sets of ten. Instruct them on proper breathing, for example, inhaling while going down, and exhaling while doing the actual push up. This teaches them that even pushups are 'whole body' exercises and teaches them mindfulness, which is transferrable to academic pursuits. Try to get them to do 50-100 and incorporate math exercises by asking them how many sets of ten they have to do to get to 50 or 100, or other age appropriate problems. Even though these are simple questions, they involve the brain and helps to keep them mentally sharp. By using multiples of 12, 15, or 17 for example, the questions can be made more challenging.

Ask the students to give feedback on how the swelling in the chest feels and discuss the physiology of blood flow as a result of muscle use. Have them observe their breath rates increasing due to the physical demands of needing more oxygen. Ask them how they 'feel' emotionally after doing pushups. Discuss physical power. Teach them how to take the radial pulse on their wrists to show how the heart has to beat faster to supply the oxygen demand required by the activity. Toward the end of the exercise session, when the students are getting tired and experiencing muscle fatigue, remind them of fortitude. Recite the definition and tell them that the adversity that they are presently experiencing is temporary and due more to mental rather than physical limitations. Teach them that fortitude means overcoming obstacles, large and small. Afterward, praise them on their efforts and review fortitude and engage them in discussion. If the teacher has martial arts training, this can be done progressively with punches, kicks, fighting combinations and simulations. Each time, this should involve experiential anatomy, math, affirmations, and lessons on fortitude.

Film Study on Fortitude

View the film, "12 Years a Slave," directed by Steve McQueen. Take notes and observe instances and examples of Solomon Northup exhibiting fortitude. Discuss other examples. Describe some of the scenes and activities that demonstrate fortitude and write a five paragraph paper entitled, "Three Examples of Fortitude in the Film, "12 years a Slave."" (See appendices 1& 2)

Experiential Exercise-Commitment

When discussing commitment, one is immediately reminded of the courageous men, women and children of the Civil Rights and Black Power Movements. One key person in those struggles was Ella Baker, who said, "Strong people don't need strong leaders." She believed in the concept of group-centered leadership and a key component of that is commitment. In this group-centered context, everyone pitches in and shares their load of leadership based on their commitment to do their part. In the classroom, this can be created by assigning a group project and allowing the students to decide who is going to do what. Their work is shared and the grade is shared and each person must commit to complete a certain part of the assignment or the whole group suffers. Another way this can be taught is to pair the students in twos and do an exercise whereby they have to rely on their partner. Facing each other, both students hold on to the outstretched arms of the other and leans back such that they are holding each other up. This works best with students about the same size and weight. The physical aspect of this exercise involves a commitment because each student must be committed or make a pledge not let go of the other person. Commitment can also be taught by having a line of students with eyes closed being led by a student with eyes open. The students with the eyes closed are making a commitment to trust the one to lead them properly around the room or yard and the student with eyes open is making a commitment to lead them safely. In both instances, commitment is combined with trust to create an experiential exercise that is easily remembered.

Experiential Exercise-Responsibility

Since we are experiencing exponential change in the arena of technology, one way to teach responsibility is to make students responsible for taking care of their classroom's instructional technology. Each classroom today is equipped with TVs, DVD players and projectors, video cameras, laptops and personal computers, calculators, and some even have ipads and Kindles for reading. A rotating crew of students can be assigned and trained to be responsible for charging, maintaining, trouble-shooting and protecting this equipment. These are valuable skills. Nowadays, corporations pay huge sums for IT personnel. Thus, students would be learning responsibility and a marketable skill at the same time. Yet, it is also experiential, involving hands-on-knowledge, problem solving, and technical know-how all combined. Additionally, other classroom tasks that are non-technical but still needed can be assigned to instill a sense of responsibility. Erasing the board, picking up paper, arranging the seats neatly, grading each other's papers, handing back papers, and collecting homework all can be viewed as tasks of responsibility. In conjunction with parents, students can be given chores at home and receive credit for doing them to increase incentive.

Another way to teach responsibility is to take the class on a field trip to an animal shelter where they have to care for and walk abandoned and homeless pets. It is probably one of the best ways to teach responsibility because it involves a living animal that can reciprocate love and affection. Students get to see first hand the positive effect they can have on various kinds of creatures and gain compassion along with responsibility. They get to witness the strong life force within all of creation and see the will and "never give up attitude" that all living creatures innately possess. Hopefully, it will help them want to make things just a little easier for someone else and prepare them to become responsible parents and fathers.

Chapter 2

Traditional Societies, Slave Culture, and The Ring Shout: Indigenous Values and African American Manhood Development

Abstract

This essay proposes that certain values and practices from traditional societies and African American slave culture can be useful as foundation practices in the development of African American manhood. Inherent in rituals such as the Ring Shout, are ideas on community, egalitarianism, and spiritual fortitude that are needed to further establish a sense of responsibility within African American men.

Introduction

Traditional societies have values and practices that could benefit people living in the modern world. Their ideas around childrearing, treatment of the elderly, and methods of conflict resolution, among others, are in some ways more advanced compared to Western oriented societies. **(1)** African American slave culture retained many practices from its native West African traditional origin. Others were an amalgamation of practices from different regions adapted to new world conditions. One of these practices became known as the 'Ring Shout.' It is recommended in this essay, that African Americans incorporate some of the best practices from traditional societies, in general, and African and African American slave culture, specifically, including the Ring

Shout, as foundation elements in developing training programs and classes for young African American men.

Traditional Societies

Jared Diamond, in his book, *The World Until Yesterday: What Can We Learn from Traditional Societies,* tells the fascinating story of his many years of interaction with traditional cultures, particularly in New Guinea. Although he is only passively critical of capitalist and colonialist disruption, genocide, and at times, ecocide, Diamond exhibits an in-depth knowledge of the rhythms and significance of traditional cultural practices. In a non-romanticized way, he relates his experiences, observations, and anecdotes covering a near fifty-year period. In the process, he has been able to observe patterns of behavior and cultural practices that could be adapted, in general, to Western lifestyles and modes of living. Fully understanding that cultural practices evolve over many years and embody the philosophical and spiritual values of a people, he nonetheless feels that certain ideas around childrearing, treatment of the elderly, and conflict resolution could be, with specific modifications, utilized in the West. **(2)**

As regards childrearing, for example, Diamond points out that traditional societies use little to no violence in disciplining their children. There is virtually no spanking in some societies. This is contrasted with the oftentimes, severe whippings and corporeal punishment within American and African American families, often administered by fathers. As outlined elsewhere (***Whose Future is It?***), it has been theorized that the brutality slaves experienced during slavery was internalized and passed

37

down in the form of beating children and domestic violence. In contrast, for some societies like the Aka traditional forest dwellers in Central Africa, violence against children is grounds for divorce. **(3)** Needless to say, violence against children in this region is rare. Therefore, it is speculated that if spankings and whippings were severely limited or eliminated within African American families, there would be less residual anger that could be passed down to future generations. The long-term affect of this could be increased closeness between parents and children and a safer community.

Another childrearing practice done by traditional societies that can be adapted is to have fathers spend more time participating in childcare. The fathers in Aka culture spend more time with their children than any other group, Western or not, in the world. Barry S. Hewlett, in ***Intimate Fathers: The Nature and Context of Aka Pygmy Paternal Infant Care*** describes:

"Due to the high availability and active caregiving of their fathers, Aka males may not be as rejecting of feminine things, such as infant care, gathering, and food preparation. ...Aka fathers do not perceive or act as though infant care has a bearing upon their masculinity, and they demonstrate intrinsic satisfaction while caregiving. **(4)**

Hewlett further explains that along with their egalitarian society, lack of violence against women, and other features of their foraging culture, there is overall more equality between the sexes in addition to more emotionally secure and stable children. **(5)**

Other features that could be helpful are the ways children play in traditional societies, commonly making their own toys, and their permission to explore and know their environments. Obviously, living in fast paced urban cities with speeding cars, gun battles, and police chases, small children cannot wander about unattended. But, within reason, young children could be taken to city, regional, and national parks, and natural preserves much more than present to explore and renew their sense of wonder and surprise. These experiences could broaden their knowledge of nature and create an innate interest in science and the natural world. This curiosity might later blossom into a science career.

The elderly in many traditional societies are cared for, respected, and needed much more than in Western cultures. Although there is wide variation, and due to extreme climates within nomadic cultures, the elderly are at times left behind to fend for themselves, by and large they are viewed with reverence and appreciation. In these cultures, they are seen as having deep repositories of knowledge and wisdom. Particularly in societies lacking computer and communications technology and literacy, Diamond explains that the elders are the main sources of knowledge and their memories serve as Google search engines, encyclopedias, and libraries for their respective cultures. Furthermore, their practical knowledge of arts, crafts, and hunting strategies are vital for survival. **(6)** In these cultures, the elderly provide a needed function by taking care of and supervising grandchildren, which adds to their self-worth. This provides them an important place in the society. Additionally, their understanding of the myths, stories, and spiritual practices along with healing incantations, herbs, and ceremonies gives them added status and prestige within their group. Children growing up in such societies have more respect for their elders. The idea of attacking, mugging, or robbing them, which happens regularly in urban America, is anathema to the core of their psyche and virtually unheard of. Many African American communities would benefit if they valued our elders as much as traditional societies do.

With regard to conflict resolution, traditional societies are practical. Living in small communities where everyone knows everyone, and understanding that the group's survival is dependent on individuals functioning as a cohesive whole, each member realizes that it is in the best interest of the group to find ways to work disagreements out amicably. They understand that warfare takes a tremendous toll on the group as a whole, and in most cases, it is better to try to find solutions. Lacking and not desiring police forces, courts, jails, and prisons and finding the idea of sequestering an individual away from their families for months or years impractical and in some ways, barbaric, traditional societies have come up with a wide variety of ways to make restitution, resolve conflicts, and ease tensions whereby people can continue to face each other daily and function. While noting that traditional societies have violent feuds, resentments, and engage in petty squabbles just as modern societies, Diamond explains that they also understand that because of their size, oft-times isolation, and dependence on the natural environment to live, they need each other and must work to maintain cohesiveness among the group. Even though there are exceptions whereby individuals are sometimes banned from the group, which amounts to a death sentence in most cases, these groups struggle to find solutions, even to capital crimes like murder. **(7)**

In a case where someone has been killed, a delicate balance of negotiating, expressing condolences, and finding appropriate restitution may take several weeks or months. Yet, the goal is to find a way whereby family pride is maintained, individual feelings acknowledged and assuaged, and group solidarity preserved. A number of animals might be exchanged, food given, or specified work agreed upon for a period of time. But the goal is always the same, to find a way to maintain social equilibrium by making sure each party, family or clan has been respected, provided for, and given a chance to request their desired form and amount of restitution. Conflict resolution is carried out to prevent warfare, which everyone realizes takes a tremendous toll on human and natural resources and detracts from their ultimate purpose, surviving against the forces of nature and their environment.

The modern practice of Restorative Justice takes many of the core principles from traditional methods of conflict resolution and applies them to modern settings, particularly urban, violence filled communities. More than any other traditional or indigenous cultural practice adapted so far, Restorative Justice techniques have garnered a small following and are being implemented in cities around the world, especially in New Zealand and the United States. In *The Spiritual Roots of Restorative Justice,* edited by Michael Hadley, the author explains the spiritual origins of restorative justice methods being used around the world:

"Restorative Justice, with its principles of repentance, forgiveness, and reconciliation, is instead a deeply spiritual process. It is never the easy way out: neither for the offender, the victim, nor the community. It requires all of us to come to grips with who we are, what we have done, and what we can become in the fullness of our humanity. It is about doing justice as if people really mattered:

41

it addresses the need for a vision of the good life, and the Common Good." **(8)**

      In restorative justice healing circles, largely drawn from traditional Maori practices of New Zealand, but adapted and transformed by local traditional practices, all of the parties involved are seated in a circle, the perpetrator of the alleged crime or violation, the victim, their respective family members, the circle leaders, and any other official personnel depending on the setting (i.e. Community center, court, jail, prison, or home.)**(9)** The circle leader states the specific reason for being there, the victim explains how or why they were wronged and the perpetrator is allowed to offer first an explanation, and then an apology. The explanation and apology may or may not be accepted and the conversation may be expanded to include other significant parties until a resolution is reached. If it is not reached in one session, then another is scheduled. In modern societies, community service, a fine, and some kind of work exchange is offered as restitution, often having the larger community act as the recipient or mediator. This often prevents the retaliation and gang warfare that could ensue after wrongs have been committed. It additionally stops a cycle of violence and death that could go on for years and lessens or serves as a substitute for a lengthy prison sentence. Just as in traditional societies, it allows people in modern urban settings who are usually from the same or adjacent neighborhoods, to function on a daily basis, peacefully.

      RJOY, or Restorative Justice for Oakland Youth in Oakland, California has become a pivotal leader in designing restorative justice solutions to inner city problems. Founded in 2005 by Fania Davis, Nancy Nadel, Aeeshah Clottey and several others, it functions as a non-profit organization giving workshop trainings in restorative justice techniques and strategies locally and nationally. They work on-site at schools resolving conflicts and mediating resolutions to gang tensions and disputes. They aim to institutionalize restorative justice throughout the schools, community, and criminal justice system and have been successful in creating a dialogue on the possibilities of restorative justice lessening the rush to criminalize and imprison so many African American youth. In Oakland, they have been able to substantially reduce school-wide violence, suspensions, and overall tension, specifically in middle schools. Instead of specific laws and punishment, RJOY and restorative justice asks three basic questions; "

"Who was harmed? What are the needs and responsibilities of all affected? How do all affected parties together address needs and repair them?" **(10)**

In each of these examples and others, traditional cultural practices have something to offer modern societies. Despite new technology, science, and modern conveniences, certain basic needs of family life have been the same for thousands of years. People need water, food, clothing of some kind (in most cases) and some kind of shelter. People need togetherness, emotional interaction, and love. The basic rules of childrearing, taking care of the elderly and conflict resolution are universal. Children have to be protected, cared for, fed, and taught. The elderly have to be cared for, listened to, and acknowledged as being integral to the society's functioning. Conflict resolution is necessary regardless if one lives in a teepee or high-rise apartment building, because if people cannot get along there is constant turmoil and stress. And no community can survive with constant upheavals and violence. Therefore, "Returning to the Source," culturally speaking is one way to facilitate the transmission of vital knowledge and specific practices of how to get along.

Africa American Slave Culture

Sterling Stuckey, Jason Young, Albert Raboteau, Alex Bontempts, Sharla Fett, and several others have written extensively on African American slave culture. No longer looked upon derisively and dismissed outright, these authors and others have shown that specific cultural practices were maintained, transformed, and created to allow African slaves a way to survive and sometimes thrive despite some of the most barbaric, brutal, inhuman treatment in history. Stuckey in his monumental work, ***Slave Culture: Nationalist Theory and the Foundations Of Black America,*** explains the thought processes underlying specific cultural practices that African slaves adapted and transformed to meet New World conditions.

"Coming from cultures in which work and art were united so completely that any notion of art for art's sake lacked meaning, Africans in North America created while working, as they had done before. For all the comparative leisure available to whites, the African used his imagination to reflect on life in the new land with an originality sufficient to bring indigenous artistic forms into being." **(11)**

Stuckey further describes the spiritual fusion of everyday activities with sacred meaning, such as giving thanks at harvest time. Africans took nothing for granted.

"At harvest time in Virginia and elsewhere, dances were held outdoors to climax the planting season, an expression of the slaves' gratefulness to forces bigger than man, to the ancestral spirits for the fertility of the soil and the renewal of the life process." **(12)**

The Africans, whose descendants would form the core of African Americans today, largely came from West and Central African cultures that had similar views toward nature, ancestral reverence, artistic expression, and ring formation rituals. Festivals like the John Kunering, essentially a series of kneeling prayers done around harvest time, universal respect for the power of the drum, the significance of certain animals and birds like the vulture or 'buzzard,' and participation in ring formation rituals like the Ring Shout stand out as unifying cultural artifacts. They gave Africans an external semblance of their experiences in Africa and internal hope for freedom and survival in a New World. These practices formed the foundation for the creation of a people comprising diverse and at times, warring societies. Yet, the commonality of the brutal slave experience coupled with a shared set of core values and rituals allowed the newly formed people to coalesce and create a set of spiritual and artistic mediums that exist unto today.

If young African American boys and men understood and practiced some of these rituals themselves, they would have a deeper sense of history and shared set of inner experiences that would allow them to see their own reflection in their brother's and sister's eyes. Furthermore, if they saw themselves in others and recognized a shared history, culture, and values, they would not be so quick to harm, shoot, and kill each other. There is not a direct relationship between cultural and spiritual awareness and a more non-violent approach to problem solving. But, coupled with an overall understanding of restorative justice type conflict resolution practices, traditional society's reverence for children and respect for the elderly, there could be a more holistic consciousness and empathy developed toward life that could translate into a more peaceful co-existence with all life forms. One key practice that could possibly lend toward that larger sensitization process is an understanding and practicing, in a modified form, of the Ring Shout.

The Ring Shout

The ring shout is arguably the oldest African American spiritual and religious ritual in North America. With the circle as the common denominator, the ring shout provided an outlet of spiritual release and mystical confirmation binding together different African cultures while solidifying a social and political bond born of a common plight, destiny and future. **(13)** While ring formation rituals form just one aspect of continental African forms of worship, they took central stage in New World, diaspora communities and were some of the few practices many diverse African cultures could agree on. **(14)** This was due to the pervasive use of circle formations in spiritual as well as social ceremonies throughout West and Central West Africa. Cultures such as the Bakongo from the Kongo, The Mende from Sierra

Leone, the Ashanti from Ghana as well as Sufi Muslims from the Senegambia area were all familiar with and had a shared understanding of its power and significance.

The circle represents the sun, moon, seasonal patterns, animal migrations, birth and death cycles and the movements of many celestial formations. It represents power, inclusiveness, something whole, comprehensive, and unified. The circle formation had been used in these cultures for thousands of years and provided a haven and sanctuary away from the rigors of ordinary life. In the New World, the circular or ring formation ritual and subsequent 'shout,' took on a more important role providing cultural tradition, somatic memory, resistance ritual, and a legitimate form of spiritual worship and mystical experience.

Done in a counterclockwise formation, the Ring Shout consists of slowly moving around a circle without crossing the feet, which was considered dancing, while bending, swaying, and rocking back and forth accompanied by selected 'shout songs.' These songs were an amalgamation of old English hymns interspersed with African interpretations and symbolism, undergirded with African rhythms and beats. It was usually done out in the woods far away from the slave owner's ears and until the 1740's, accompanied by the drum. Later, after it was discovered that these gatherings served multiple purposes such as meetings for slave revolts, insurrections, and sabotage, as well as spiritual rejuvenation, these meetings were then held under strict supervision in 'Praise houses,' under the watchful eye of either a slave owner or overseer. **(15)** In these cases, any covert meanings had to be encoded in the lyrics and the songs and movements took on a more layered and textured presentation.

47

The Ring Shout often produced trance like experiences and according to Stuckey, provided authentic representations of African spirituality. But the participants were not allowed to 'fallout,' or exhibit outward, demonstrative signs of their trance, like they could in Africa. Theirs was more of an inward state sensed only by those who had experienced it themselves. Based on the work of scholars like Felicitas Goodman, it could have provided them with present-time experiential awareness of their inner state of being while helping them temporarily transcend the body and their slave experience. **(16)** Furthermore, it could have given them glimpses of what the Sufis call, 'certainty,' or an assuredness of life after death and the existence or God, or Allah. **(17)** This knowledge could have given them increased faith and the strength needed to face another day of back-bending labor, unrelenting heat, and oftentimes, brutal treatment.

If young African American men learned and practiced the Ring Shout, even in a modified form, it could serve as a rite of passage ritual similar to ones done in masonic or college fraternities and other 'secret societies' by creating a shared, somatic experience and frame of reference. This shared experience could lend toward feelings of brotherhood, camaraderie, and solidarity. If these kinds of bonds are forged, they will kill each other less and be more apt to help and assist each other more. This would form a natural bridge to studying and working together, and living in close community with one another in harmony.

Conclusion

The significance of traditional indigenous culture, African American Slave culture, and the Ring Shout specifically as they pertain to African American manhood training is that they anchor young men to traditions that are rooted in history going back as far as 70,000 years. Recent research has shown that the San Bushmen of the Kalahari Desert practiced rituals devoted to the python snake during this time. **(18)** This predates the previous known estimates of worship by more than 30,000 years. If young African American men understood that they were connected to rituals that were old and continuously practiced along with other time tested practices and values of traditional culture, they would be given guidelines and principles that supersede the crass materialism and conspicuous consumption of Western Civilization and America. And according to noted Psychologist and African centered thinker, Dr. Wade Nobles, these kinds of rituals would rescue them from or at least mitigate Western thinking, characterized by an emphasis on individualism, competitiveness, and secular, scientific and materialistic paradigms.

Additionally, by viewing themselves through the long lens of ancient history, they would be able to raise their self-esteem and realize they are not who they think they are, down trodden, poor, urban city dwellers, pitted against one another in a dog eat dog fight for survival. Neither would they be given the pipe dream of being 'Kings and Queens of Africa,' an oppressive notion at best. They would be given the realistic concept that they were and are part of the original people of humanity, practicing cultural practices and rituals handed down from antiquity that teach respect for nature, animals, and humans. With this foundation, they could develop a reverence for all of creation, living and non-living, not the least of which are their own African American brothers and sisters.

Review Questions

1. Where are your parents, grandparents, and great grandparents from? How far back can you trace your roots? Do you know of any family traditions or customs handed down in your family? What have you learned from them?

2. Do you know your grandparents or great grandparents? How are they treated and cared for? Do you remember details about them, birth and or death dates, how they dressed, looked, smelled, walked, talked, laughed-things of everyday life? (*Look up family members on ancestry.com and begin a genealogical search. Do the DNA test. Use it as a family project*)

3. Do you have any experience in your family of living communally? Do any of your relatives live in the south? What are some of the communal customs they brought with them? Food? Speech? Funerals, births?

4. Have you ever planted or worked in a garden? Describe some of those experiences.

5. Do you know any folktales from the Southern U.S.? Any superstitions passed down within your family? Discuss how folktales, superstitions and stories passed down through generations express oral wisdom and cultural memory. Why is this important?

Classroom Exercise: Film Study

Show Haile Gerima's film, "Sankofa." Use the film to illustrate the importance of the Sankofa concept, "return and fetch it," as it relates to incorporating aspects of traditional practices into Western culture. Discuss how the film's imagery, specific scenes, and dialog convey the relationship of African to African-American culture. What archetypal meaning can be assessed to the characters of Nunu, Shango, Mona, Shola, Joe, and others as they relate to modern day African Americans? Compare the ceremony of the slaves in the film to the description of the Ring Shout

Writing Exercise

*Write a five-paragraph essay entitled, "**Three Examples of "Return and Fetch it" in the film Sankofa.**" The essay should have an introduction, three body paragraphs (one example each), and a conclusion. There should be four to six sentences per paragraph with the three examples outlined in the thesis sentence in the introduction. Read aloud or discuss. (See Appendix 2)*

Somatic Exercise: Ring Shout

Get in a circle. Put on the "Georgia Sea Island Singers" cd of shout songs. Moving counterclockwise, step sideways without overlapping the feet. As you move around the circle begin to gently sway from side to side. To create an internal state of worship, gently chant under your breath the name of the creator. Chant gently, Allah, Allah, or God, God, or Yahweh, Yahweh, or Hare Krishna, Hare Krishna or Nam-myoho-renge-kyo, Nam-myoho-renge-kyo, or any number of indigenous chants. At first, perform for only thirty minutes. As time goes on, repeat with more original steps, incorporating contemporary dance moves like turf dancing to provide an original somato-emotional release ritual for each group.

Chapter 3

Political Consciousness: A Prerequisite for African American Manhood

Abstract

Political Consciousness, in a broad, holistic context is needed to enable African American men the ability to navigate 21st century American economic, cultural, and political terrain with insight and intellectual dexterity. This essay will outline some of the multifaceted aspects of what is required to be politically conscious in a post-industrial, automated, technologically advanced world and why it is a prerequisite for African American manhood.

Introduction

Political consciousness is a prerequisite to real manhood because manhood involves responsibility, and without political consciousness, one does not know what one should be responsible for. What one should be responsible for is oneself, one's family, and if truly responding to the needs of the time, the larger community and planet. Furthermore, this consciousness will enable one to do three things; understand and withstand the arrows and barbs of racism and white supremacy, inspire deep contemplation, and empower one to become politically active.

Political Study and Street Knowledge

To be politically conscious as an African American man, one must first study the historical and political forces that have led up to today's situation. By studying the forces stacked against African Americans and other oppressed groups in America as well as the countless struggles to overcome them, one realizes that there are historical patterns and deeply entrenched attitudes that keep racism, white supremacy, and implicit bias in place. Things are not the way they are by accident, but by design. It is related to the desire for profit, power, and continued privilege. It also requires study of the futuristic direction that the world and America are headed in terms of Science and Technology. Since the fifties, thinkers such as Daniel Bell, James Boggs, Sidney M. Willhelm, Alvin Toffler and others have been critically looking at the relationship of automation and cybernation to the loss of industrial and manufacturing jobs in urban America. (1) What is the impact of this to African American people? How does this change relate to its men? And, if one cannot work to provide an income for one's family, what should one do?

These questions are crucial because they relate directly to the war on drugs and high rates of incarceration. With high unemployment rates in inner cities, African American men often seek income by choosing to 'hustle' and work within the underground economy doing illicit and illegal activities. These illicit and illegal activities then land a high percentage of African American men in prison. Additionally, African American men must educate themselves on how nanotechnology, robotics, genetic engineering, synthetic biology, 3-D printing and other technologies impact and change society and how this correlates to the lack of low-skilled jobs. These technologies have far less human involvement. Additionally, the maintenance that is needed to keep these technologies running requires highly skilled labor with extensive education and training. By their design, with artificial intelligence doing the thinking and robotics providing the muscle, the jobs that are and will be available are in design, implementation, and management. Are members of the African American community stepping up and providing these kinds of training opportunities for young African American men and women? It is obvious that the larger society has not.

Despite the larger forces that increase one's chances of going to jail and prison, African American men must understand that sometime it is the 'little things' that initially get them in trouble and subsequently under the scrutiny of law enforcement. Understanding that police forces are able to keep up to 80% of the property that they confiscate on the street, police are constantly looking for 'probable cause,' to stop young African American and Latino men in particular. They are hustling, too. Therefore, simple things like brake and tail lights being broken, expired license plates and tags, not having a driver's license or insurance, unpaid child support, old warrants on parking tickets and other violations all are minor infractions that can easily escalate into someone being arrested, searched, imprisoned, or killed. The general rule on the street when dealing with law enforcement is, "the quicker, the better." One wants the encounter to be over as quickly as possible. The longer the encounter, the increased chance that something could go wrong and when it does, it invariably is not good for the young African American or Latino man or woman involved. Our young adults would be wise to take care of these details before driving and being in the street. If walking or taking public transportation, one should maintain current identification, avoid carrying firearms or long knives, and refrain from drinking publically or while driving. Also, in today's world, young African American men must avoid hanging out in parked cars or on street corners as the majority of drive-by shootings, random or not, occur in those situations. This type of understanding does not require sophisticated political consciousness, just Street Smarts 101. If one has both, a basic street sense and political consciousness, one is far more prepared to navigate the urban streets of America and decrease one's chances of being incarcerated. Of course, the police can harass African Americans of all classes, particularly men, at any time. There are many racist individuals in positions of power in America. But if one takes care of the details outlined above, it increases the possibility that the encounter with law enforcement will be short and one can be on their way. Ultimately, young African American and Latino men need meaningful employment, internships, travel experiences, education, and apprenticeships to completely side step the temptations of the illegal underground economy. That responsibility lies with the society at large and us.

A major reason to avoid going to jail or getting arrested for minor infractions is that when and if one really has to take a stand politically and get arrested for civil disobedience, direct action or more radical actions, one will have to only deal with that politically motivated offense. Otherwise, the penalties will be more severe and one's political activities will be hampered by spending all of one's money, or oftentimes parent's or other's money, to stay out of jail, or worse, prison. This is how many individuals, organizations and movements get bogged down with legal fees and distractions. Therefore, keeping a clean record for as long as possible *becomes strategic politically*. There are some causes that are worth getting arrested for, going to prison for, and even dying for, *but they are few* and one must clearly understand the long-term consequences of each and every action. This is all a vital part of studying the racial and legal history of America because when one does, one realizes the seriousness of engaging in political struggle and the need to be very calculating, focused, and careful in one's activities. There is a need for boldness, courage, and foresight, backed by calm deliberation to avoid recklessness. Recklessness and cavalier behavior in political struggle against the racist forces of America can get oneself and others killed.

Contemplation

After systematic study, African American men need to take time and reflect and contemplate what all of the above means in relationship to humanity as a whole. Philosopher, activist, and revolutionary thinker, Grace Lee Boggs, believes that contemplation as well as in-depth conversations around ideas are vital in clearly understanding the deeper philosophical significance of current political events. She believes that without this deep reflection and contemplation, human beings are little more than instinctively reactionary creatures responding to immediate needs and circumstances. (2) Deep reflection is needed in order to have a grasp on the future and to dialogue intelligently about it. African Americans, and its men, must be a part of this dialogue. What does the future hold for African Americans? What does the future hold for indigenous people? What does global warming, the destruction of the environment, and the lack of clean drinkable water mean for human survival? There have been five catastrophic extinctions of plants and animals during the earth's existence, with the last one being the dinosaurs. How does the sixth extinction of plant and animal species presently taking place relate to the survival and development of African American people? All of these issues have deeply political and philosophical components and in critically analyzing our political situation it helps to look at the big picture. The big picture involves the planet, science, and knowledge of the expanding universe. Political thinking, deep reflection, and philosophical contemplation form the platform and foundation for spiritual understanding around the ultimate questions of mortality, the meaning of life, purpose, and death.

Political Action

After study and contemplation, action is needed. The political action of today needs to be according to one's ability, time, and capacity. There is no one formula that fits everyone. Some may be able to be full time grassroots community organizers. Others may be facilitators within progressive non-profit organizations or established worker owned cooperatives. Some may be radical revolutionaries on the front lines protesting oil sands fracking in Canada, or on the streets of urban America occupying Wall Street and Multi-national corporations, working to dismantle dams or working with homeless youth, drug addicted individuals, helping to prevent teenage prostitution and human trafficking or assisting un-wed mothers. Still others may be working with young African American, Native, and Latino men trying to prevent them from returning to prison and help them gain meaningful education and employment. There are so many ways to become involved. Creating meaningful art through painted murals, conscious music, street and guerilla theatre, filmmaking, or providing child care, urban gardening, picking up trash, visiting and helping the elderly, campaigning for progressive political candidates, writing, teaching, healing, or donating money to meaningful causes, can all be political acts. Taking time to have an in-depth conversation about life, in this day of social media and increased alienation, is a progressive, revolutionary activity. Facilitating dialogue amongst progressive groups is an increasingly political and innovative act. Dialogue increases consciousness and whenever consciousness is raised, people's imagination of what their possibilities are increases. Hope is generated.

The idea is to live the alternative, progressive, revolutionary life in the present and change from the inside out. It is not about taking state power, but in a coordinated, federated, and organized way, eroding the power the state has over us. It is about controlling ourselves-controlling our lives. Like the Zapatistas in Chiapas, Mexico, the goal is autonomy and self-determination. This is in line with the best of African American struggle drawing its lessons from the participatory democracy of Ella Baker and the grassroots organizing of SNCC, the Black Panther Party, and countless others in the Black Power/Liberation, Black Arts and Left Movements of the sixties and seventies on to today.

Much of today's political action is also about taking lessons from and following the example of indigenous based movements and the 'global south.' People are finally realizing that indigenous communities have much to share with the world at large and their systems of egalitarianism, equality, respect for the environment, sustainability, and spiritual consciousness are needed to restore balance to a world overly imbued with materialism and technology. Instead of attempting to be vanguards, thinkers are suggesting the idea of 'accompanying' as an alternative metaphor for encouraging and bringing about social change. Historian Staughton Lynd quotes Dr. Paul Farmer,

"To accompany someone is to go somewhere with him or her, to break bread together, to be present on a journey with a beginning and an end." **(3)**

He continues by saying,

"There's an element of mystery, of openness, in accompaniment. I'll go with you and support you on your journey wherever it leads. I'll keep you company and share your fate for a while. And by "a while," I don't mean a little while. Accompaniment is much more about sticking with a task until it's deemed completed by the person or people being accompanied, rather than by the accompagnateur." **(4)**

Conclusion

The idea of accompanying signals a paradigm shift that embodies the attitude of cooperativeness and egalitarianism in struggle. It seeks to restore indigenous ideas of collective forms of leadership in political action. If young African American men adopt this kind of attitude, not just in political activities, but also in life in general, they can cease the 'every man for himself' attitude so prevalent on the street. In this way, there is no separation between political activism and life. It is a seamless whole.

In an essay titled *"Leaders Walking Backwards: Male Ex-Gang Members Perspectives and Experiences,"* Native American grandmother and professor, Alanaise Goodwill, describes the need for humility in life and how it develops a sense of responsibility. She refers to a set of teachings from her people known as the Teachings of the Seven Grandfathers. She writes,

"Another of the Seven Grandfathers focuses on humility, or daabaazandizowin. It is a very important teaching about leveling oneself and not talking down to others. Many of the men spoke about the significance of ceremony and described the process of entering a circle where no one person was elevated above another, where the teaching of daabaazandizowin is embodied. They related how humility incited feelings of responsibility for others in the circle and in their families." **(5)**

This is why political consciousness is about taking responsibility and is a prerequisite for calling oneself a whole man. Even though the racial and legal historical forces arrayed against African American people and men in particular are formidable, the ultimate responsibility to transform self and society lies with each individual working on themselves in unison with their families, community and planet. It is taking responsibility to recognize and identify these forces through concerted study internally and externally, to contemplate on the deeper meanings of these forces and one's self development, and then humbly putting oneself in situations where one has to work together with others to accomplish goals for the group as a whole. It is about understanding and respecting the rights of women, children, and animals, and allowing the more tender aspects of our selves to manifest without thinking our manhood is being thwarted or threatened. And it is about taking the ultimate responsibility of challenging the most powerful nation on earth to erase its contradictions, re-write its constitution, and transform itself into a real democracy. This is the result of real political consciousness. This is real manhood.

Review Questions

1. Have you ever participated in a political protest? What was the issue? What were the objectives of the protest? Were the objectives met?

2. What are some of the major political issues of today? How does each political issue named affect you personally? Do you feel like your "voice" or political perspective is heard? Why or why not?

3. What does political consciousness mean to you? Does it mean the same as it did back in the sixties? Why or why not? Where is this 'consciousness' located? Mind? Body?

4. Reflect on the phrases, 'live the alternative in the present,' 'be the change,' and, 'we are the leaders we have been waiting for.' What do these phrases mean to you? How do these phrases reflect a different philosophy as regards current social change strategies as compared to the sixties and seventies?

5. What is the significance of today's movements incorporating indigenous concepts such as 'seven generations,' 'egalitarianism,' 'group decision-making and leadership' into the strategic thinking process of present-day movements? What were some of the mistakes and or inconsistencies of past movements? How might this more 'horizontal' approach to social change correct past errors? What are some of the shortcomings and weaknesses in the current approach and how might they be corrected?

Classroom or Workshop Exercise: Film Study

View the Films, "Black Power Mixtape," "Angela Davis: Free the Political Prisoners," "The Trials of Muhammad Ali," "Freedom Summer," and "Mumia Abu Jamal: Long Distance Revolutionary." These five films illustrate African American political consciousness raising from a historical perspective. After viewing each film, write a five-paragraph essay explaining three significant ideas or facts learned. See Appendix 2.

Somatic Exercise-Standing Meditation

In Chinese medicine, the goal is the have 'chi,' or the spiritual life force or energy smoothly flowing through the 'meridians.' These meridians run in ten equally proportioned 'lines' up and down and within the body. Chi Gong has developed a series of standing postures to cultivate and balance 'chi' in the body. One such practice is 'Bear Pose.'

Stand with the feet directly under the shoulders, slightly bent at the knee. Raise the arms as if holding a large beach ball just under eye level. With fingertips almost touching in the front, form a large circle (as if holding the beach ball). Close your eyes. On inhalation, feel/imagine/visualize your chi or breath beginning in your left fingertips and circulating through the left arm to the middle of your chest. As you begin to exhale, feel/imagine/visualize your chi or breath circulating through your right arm out of your fingers. Then inhale and repeat, creating a circular movement of the 'chi' through the heart area and out. This is the first of many poses used to circulate 'chi.' Hold Five minutes. How does it feel?

Chapter 4

The Stress of Political Consciousness

Abstract

Political Consciousness is essential and vital in the development of African American men and women. Yet, it can be stressful. The self-imposed set of social and political responsibilities along with new awareness of historical and political realities may leave one temporarily paralyzed by euphoria, anger, fear, depression, and anxiety. To prevent and alleviate this, a holistic lifestyle grounded in political activism is recommended that offers positive outlets for expression along with personal practices for effective stress reduction.

Introduction

While there are many books and studies on the political and social ramifications of the Civil Rights, Black Power/Liberation, Black Arts and other movements of the past, there are few if any studies that chronicle the effects of the stress that derived from political involvement in those movements. The stress was a hidden factor and if political activists had been aware of this stress it would have siphoned off much of the drive and energy to make social change happen. But it was there and there was a price to be paid by being politically conscious, radical, and African American. For those of us born in the fifties and earlier, it was understood that political activism, even of a conservative kind like voter registration, could cost one their life. Therefore, the issue of stress or at least, 'lesser stressors,' have not been the burning issue. Staying alive was the burning issue.

But for the ones who survived, how did the stress of political consciousness and activism impact them? How many lost jobs at different times? Did that cause any stress in the family? How did that affect family member's health? Did people have to move and relocate because of their activities? Did one ever have to go 'underground?' How long? For how many years did one have to 'bite their tongue' at work and where did that frustrated anger go? Or if they were of the sort that 'didn't bite their tongue,' did the resultant conflicts prevent them from advancing? Were there careers that one would have gone into had one not been politically conscious of certain things and took certain actions? *Of course, the larger question of how different our lives would have been had not millions stood up and demanded justice has an obvious answer. And in every struggle there are numerous sacrifices to be made and each generation has to step up to the need of the times.* Yet, we seldom discuss the collateral damage of lives lost, years in prison, or sapped potential sucked away by sometimes misguided actions, racist police, courts and criminal justice systems, federally instigated internecine battles, and ideological wars. In many ways, the people making the sacrifices did not know they were making sacrifices at the time and could not foresee the outcomes. Neither could people foresee the lasting effects of stress on their and their family's nervous systems and how that would affect them years later.

These are hard realities and questions. But ultimately, if we can not assure an individual that they will be taken care of when they get old, their loved ones cared for if something happens to them or will be nursed when they are sick, why should they choose to join our struggle? It is now acknowledged amongst activists and scholars alike that it will take generations to fully usher in any kind of advanced society. Nothing short of catastrophic disasters will make people change instantly, *so it comes down to how well an individual can hold up and possibly thrive under an assortment of pressures over a very long period of time*. The Communist Party and Progressive Movement of the teens, twenties, and thirties, the Civil Rights movement of the forties and fifties, and the Black Power/Liberation, student and Black Arts Movements of the sixties and seventies were accompanied by support systems that were created within those movements. This helped mitigate and insulate the frontline activists from some of the stressors, particularly financial. The Civil Rights workers also had broad-based support within the African American community. But, there is another reality. Many individuals who chose a life of political activism, especially radical African American political activism, lived lonely existences, particularly as they got older. They could not find work. They made a lot of sacrifices personally and professionally while incurring tremendous stress to their nervous systems. Today, many have poor health. Few offer any regrets as to their choices politically, but many feel the pain of isolation, lack of appreciation, and the toll the movement has taken on their bodies, psyches and spirits.

The happiest ones seemed to have found a balance, an internal peace knowing that they gave it their all and have a lifetime of achievements and accomplishments, big and small, to show for the paths they took. They also have had a certain measure of good fortune and luck, as most have shared that there were many instances, where they were in very dangerous situations that that could have gone 'either way.' Today, they have healthy pursuits, activities, and relationships and live within a community. And, they are still politically active and vibrant. Despite political victories being few and far between, they know it was the correct path. But how did they get to this point? How did they find equilibrium? How did they balance the stress of being aware and politically active, with working and paying bills, or raising families?

The mainstream perspective, one that teaches us that America is a just nation, has altruistic motives with regards the peoples, nations and resources of the planet, and is a real democracy where legal, economic, and political justice prevails, is not the reality for the majority. So, what happens when those blinders are removed? And then, how well does one manage those stressors once they 'see the light?' More specifically, what are some of the powerful emotional states triggered by becoming politically aware and how do they produce unhealthy situations and symptoms for individuals if not identified and remedied? This is the purpose of this essay, to identify several distinct emotional states that often arise within the political consciousness-raising phase that if identified, could possibly be mitigated and managed in a healthy, holistic way.

Stressful Stages of Political Consciousness

The states outlined below are not always experienced in a linear fashion. Neither is this a scientific study or analysis based on research. These are still needed. The following ideas are based on forty-five years of direct participation and observation, talking with numerous contacts and conversations with hundreds of activists, some who have lived nine decades or more, and personal experiences spanning more than fifty years.

Euphoria

In many cases, euphoria or euphoria-like feelings are the first strong emotions that arise when one first becomes politically conscious. This is because one feels as if his/her consciousness has been liberated. Whether the awareness emerges from consciousness around race, class, gender, the environment, poverty, hunger, sexuality, capitalism, science and technology, indigenous rights, there is often an elation and exhilaration that comes from understanding something anew or phenomena becoming illumined from a new perspective. When an influential book, event, film, lecture, class, or a large scale demonstration, police or national guard attack, overseas war, epiphany about life, or an accumulation of all the above in an instant or over a period of time, grabs one's attention, one's consciousness expands and one sees things as if for the first time. New political awareness heightens one's observation skills and one begins to think more critically, analyze more effectively, and in many respects, feel more alive. Politically conscious people feel excited. Even children of long-time activists who grew up with politically conscious dialogue often have their own awakening based on their unique life experiences. This euphoria gives a great deal of energy and fuels a passion for reading, discussing, creating, organizing, and living out new political realities.

Yet, it can be destabilizing as well. If one is not careful, one can begin to view all of life and relationships through the newfound political lens and depending on one's personal skills and personality, or lack thereof, make a real nuisance of oneself. One can become overbearing in the beginning because one may have a tendency to try to 'teach' every person one encounters while being prone to long political discourses. Sometimes there is self-righteousness during this time that if magnified in a group context, can erupt into political turf battles. **(1)** If these political transformations are accompanied by diet and other changes and experimentation, it could leave the young person additionally imbalanced.

It is better to have a gradual shift, or at least a well thought out transition in lifestyles, diets, and political beliefs and affiliations. The idea is to channel this initial euphoria into an integrative plan of how political awareness and knowledge can be woven effectively and smoothly into one's life. In this way, it can be part and parcel of one's being for an entire lifetime. Turn euphoria into productive enthusiasm, excitement and work.

Anger

Anger is a logical emotional response to becoming politically conscious. This process often involves historical study, and depending on one's starting point, i.e. African American, Native, Latino, or Asian American, women, LGBTI, the environment, workers, indigenous rights or other ways to view political reality, the historical picture is filled with horror, pain, and vast devastation. When one reads how African slaves were marched through hundreds of miles of dense, disease ridden vegetation and swamps in Africa and beaten while barely being fed, watching their loved ones die, one's stomach turns in sympathetic grief and agony and one gets angry. When one reads of how Pizarro tricked the Incan ruler and mercilessly killed him and all of his family and massacred his people, one gets angry. When one reads or sees a film depicting slavery in all of its brutality, like, "*Twelve Years a Slave*," for example, one can not help but ache and commiserate, at least in some small way, with the suffering of African enslaved women, children, and men. When one hears about the mutilated fingers, hands, and arms of present-day Latino migrant workers without insurance or legal rights in U.S. meatpacking houses and the conditions of both immigrant and migrant workers in general, one gets angry. When people see images of dogs brutally attacking African American marchers, or worse, read about the Wounded Knee Massacre in South Dakota, where over 300 Lakota men, women, and children were gunned down by U.S. soldiers in 1894, they get angry, and want to fight back. Historical events like these make a person angry and when one begins to understand the systematic nature and economic/religious underpinnings of racism, slavery, and today's white supremacy, one gets angry. Many years ago, reading **The Wretched of the Earth,** by Franz Fanon, made people angry and more aware of how anger could be translated into power through revolutionary struggle. **(2)**

Learning about injustice naturally strikes a cord of sympathy, particularly among young adults, and this sympathy can produce an anger that can, at times, backfire. It can make the person feel a sense of urgency that is not based in reality. They may feel that a particular political act is worth 'risking everything' for and in that moment they feel it is the only time they can do it in their life. In reality, there are very few of those moments. What

72

there is, is the oft-times dull reality of daily life, and the less glamorous aspects of struggle, like organizing, distributing information, direct action disruptions and demonstrations, addressing issues, teaching, facilitating, fundraising, and or supporting progressive candidates. The idea is to "live to fight another day."

For example, since the police are shooting young African American males, some young activists, might feel justified in randomly shooting police. There are several arguments and ways to approach this issue and one argument asks, *"Can you defeat an enemy using the same tactics they are using against you?"* and *"Are police really the enemy?"* Another argument is, *"Fight fire with fire,"* others say, *"that to fully evolve, one must use political tactics and strategies and put them ahead of military ones because military ones are extremely costly in terms of human life."* **(3)** But, *"where does that put self-defense when one is defending oneself against the police or the "state?"* Or, *"what are the ramifications of openly declaring warfare against the police? What political purpose does it serve?"* This is an example of the kind of dialogue a newly politically conscious person needs to hear early on and participate in such that he or she can have an intellectual context to analyze their anger before acting on it out of haste. Of course, many events happen so quickly at times, there is not a lot of time for deliberation. But today, if people joining organizations, movements, study groups, or political classes are informed beforehand that the material and issues being discussed might bring up various emotions, including anger, and they are informed that these emotions are normal responses, people would more easily be able to integrate the information, their new political views, and extreme feelings and emotions generated by this new endeavor. Ultimately, this will make for more productive individuals and activists long term that choose their actions carefully.

Depression

The depression that can accompany political consciousness and activity is more than likely not actual clinical depression, in most cases, unless it tips the person in a direction that unmasks a predisposition. But there is, at times, the possibility of feeling like having an extra weight on one's shoulders, that is, the 'weight of the world,' in addition to the ups and downs of everyday life itself. The individual may suddenly feel emotionally overwhelmed by all of the 'new' information and appalled at the brutal historical past of the United States. In past social struggles, the issues were very clear in terms of voting, equal rights, removal of Jim Crow, ending the war and women and gay rights. They did not have to address or acknowledge huge overarching problems such as global pandemics, specie extinction, climate change and environmental degradation looming forever in the background like today. This is in addition to social/political struggles of immense proportions. With more being on the table and people having conjoined issues and perspectives, it seems like there is more to get depressed about today. Of course, in the past, people were depressed about economic collapse, getting lynched or being shot.

It is vital that each person stays connected with their community, or form new ones, and is proactive. Live communally, if possible. By living communally or in the context of community, one is around people to converse and laugh with. Human beings are very social creatures and interaction produces a wide range of emotional states. Rarely would an entire group be depressed all at the same time.

Another remedy is staying focused on doing things, no matter how small, to alleviate the identified social problems to one's capacity. Putting forth positive solutions keeps one preoccupied with the work rather than personal problems and small successes encourage a more hopeful outlook. This eventually becomes a pattern that can lift one's mood. It is similar to Morita Therapy in Japan, the individual focuses on 'doing what needs doing' by staying 'present in the moment.' (4) In this way, the new activist is encouraged and stimulated to cultivate a more positive outlook and approach, based on immediately positive experiences, despite global circumstances. This is in line with the current idea of living the alternative in the present.

Anxiety

Often, newfound political consciousness, particularly of a radical kind questioning the economic, racial, gender, and environmental foundation of Western Civilization while incorporating Indigenous Rights, challenges the 'status quo.' Challenging the status quo can make one, at times, anxious, or have anxiety, which is defined as, "*uneasiness and apprehension, as about future uncertainties.*" (5) Anxiety causes one to worry. Yet, it is normal to feel anxious when one is about to embark on a road of uncertainty in unexplored territory. At least today's activists have a historical roadmap that can be used to alert present-day and future activists about possible pitfalls and ways to avoid obvious mistakes. But, each era or movement has its own unique set of historical circumstances that must be respected, assessed and studied. Once one realizes the immensity of the task, and the tremendous amount of attention the State or 'powers that be' can bring to bear to prosecute and or destroy a targeted activist or movement, one might become anxious.

Much of this anxiety, however, is experienced as long as one feels alone and isolated. If one views their situation collectively and avoids the individualism so prevalent today, the anxiety or worry created by thinking one is taking on huge corporations, prison-industrial complexes, and global entities by oneself, is lessened. **(6)** Planning one's career such that it incorporates aspects of one's political work could relieve additional anxiety. In this way, the political work is embedded in the Life's work, since a great deal of the anxiety comes from not knowing how one's future success will be affected by taking and acting on one's political beliefs. Today's non-profits partially help by providing income for doing organizational and political work.

Yet, there still may be sacrifices to be made. In the twenties and thirties, the sacrifices were extreme. Communist Party hierarchy would accuse an individual of 'careerism' if they put their careers before the work of the Party. Members were made to feel that the only really important work was the political work of the Party, and their personal lives were secondary. This same tendency could be seen in Black Nationalist groups in the sixties and seventies as well. Today's movements would benefit from a more inclusive platform and holistic critique. Knowing that the objectives of a just, progressive, and sustainable/durable society might take many years to implement, it is now recognized, even within radical political circles, that people need personal and inner fulfillment, too. Young activists' anxiety might be reduced greatly if they could see a vision of themselves participating in meaningful political work and rewarding careers at the same time.

Fear

Taking on and challenging, the foundations of power in America, as represented by the huge financial interests of Wall Street and its military, scientific, and philanthropic tentacles worldwide, is an awesome task. Even thinking about it can produce feelings of immense fear. If forces of power are making huge sums of money, be they private or governmental, and another group is saying that the way they are handling business, particularly in how they are evaluating and determining worth and distributing wealth is unfair; and also saying that they are not sustainable and equitable-they are at odds. Anyone who is at odds with capitalism, is in the way, and should be fearful. In looking at the past, one can immediately see the stream of bodies of people who have gotten in its way. History has shown that the risks of life and limb are real, with variations of intensity and tension at different periods.

People who get involved in political work are not just fearful for themselves, but their families, too. During the McCarthy era of Communist witch-hunts, many family members lost government and other jobs because of hear say and innuendo. So, depending on the circumstances and historical situation, if one finds oneself in a frightening circumstance, what is one to do?

Paul Robeson, was in such a situation in June 1956 when he was asked to testify in front of the House of Un-American Affairs or HUAC. He was a world famous actor, singer, lawyer, and activist and the United States government had taken away his passport. He frequently had traveled to the Soviet Union and many other countries around the world and explained to audiences the plight and struggle of the American Negro. For someone of Robeson's stature to openly embrace radical politics, communism, and befriend the Soviet Union was extraordinary and threatening. Furthermore, William L. Patterson, and several others, had written a searing history of lynching and racially based murder titled, **We Charge Genocide**, which Robeson helped personally deliver to the United Nations in 1951. **(7)** This incredible document, which outlined by name hundreds who had been lynched with a complete breakdown by state, indicted the U.S. government in entirety. So, Robeson knew and worked with many communists. And although he knew many in the Communist Party, he was not himself, a member. But, he refused to 'give up his friends,' or name names. In fact, he was combative, defiant, and memorably angry in his response at the hearings. Robeson, when asked why he didn't stay in the Soviet Union, said,

"Because my father was a slave, and my people died to build this country, and I am going to stay here, and have a part of it just like you. And no fascist-minded people will drive me from it, is that clear?" **(8)**

Robeson exhibited courage in the face of fear and adversity, and it inspired generations. His pointed, direct comments given in his deep, baritone voice rang out like a scorching hymnal of indictment of this nation's treatment of his people. Whereas many others, including Langston Hughes, had withered under the pressure, he took the opportunity to show, in a David versus Goliath way, how one person can overcome their fear and face adversity.

It is very similar to confronting a bully-sometimes one has to overcome their fear and fight. Once fought, bullies often turn out not to be as tough as expected. In the early 19th century, abolishing slavery seemed impossible. The institution appeared invincible and the task insurmountable, yet, with much sacrifice and struggle, it was abolished. It took many years, and things are still not equal, but women did receive the right to vote. Although it took an additional seventy-five years, many assassinations and lynchings, court cases, and wars, Jim Crow was defeated and crushed. The LGBTI community has suffered many indignities and cruelty, yet their rights are increasingly being recognized, and in many states, same sex couples can get legally married. (9) The environment is being destroyed by capitalist greed but millions are now involved in preserving it and devising sustainable solutions.

People can initiate change if they overcome their fear. Fear does not mean stop. It means, *'proceed with caution,'* but one must keep moving forward. The best way to deal with fear is to acknowledge it and still proceed to do what one has set out to do. The fear is recognized as a normal component, even healthy component at times, that will make one careful. The key is to turn fear into careful optimism that is decisive. The optimism and courage developed in the face of political oppression is the kind of hard-earned strength and tenacity that serves one in all of life's endeavors.

Balancing it All Out

These stages are not in anyway fixed or linearly experienced. Also, there are possibly many more emotions that are experienced as well. The point is to recognize and acknowledge that each process or transformation causes a cascade of changes, internally and externally, that can be overwhelming and difficult to manage at times. If grassroots organizers were equipped with this knowledge, they could plan training workshops that address these types of issues head on. That way, the participant would be spared some growing pains and eased into various roles and responsibilities for which they have a higher capacity to carry out successfully. Hopefully, this could be done while engaged in activities that aid their personal and professional development at the same time.

So, how is all of this balanced out or integrated into the working life of an individual? What are some additional tools that could help soften the edge and jolt of new political consciousness and activity and lessen stress? Here are some suggestions.

Become a Student of History

By studying History and revolutions, as well as the life stories of ordinary people who lived during extraordinary times, one can learn of the personal sacrifices and inner struggles certain individuals made during different time periods. This information is important because it shows historical patterns and cycles as well as individual responses to different stressful situations. Biographies in particular, as well as autobiographies, are very helpful in understanding how historical events swept people up and how these otherwise ordinary people responded in extraordinary ways.

Read Tom Paine and learn about the early American Revolutionary ideals (and contradictions.) Do research on Toussaint L'Overture and Dessalines in Haiti in 1804, Louise Michel and the Paris Commune of 1871, the Russian Revolution of 1917, Spain in 1937, the Mau Mau in Kenya, the ANC and PAC in South Africa, Kwame Nkrumah in Ghana, Fidel, Che', and the Cuban Revolution, Patrice Lumumba in the Congo, Amilcar Cabral in Guinea Bissau and Cape Verde, Mao in China, Ho in Vietnam, Harriet Tubman, Frederick Douglass, and John Brown and their fight against slavery in the U.S., and the struggles of the fifties, sixties, and seventies. Study the stories of the Black Liberation Movement's rank and file. Familiarize yourself with Bayard Rustin and the ideas of Audre Lorde and June Jordan. Read about the life and times of Angela Davis. These people, historical events and stories are inspiring, but more importantly, they are instructive. They are a good study for anyone interested in civil rights and revolutionary struggles of the past.

One book that covers most 20th century revolutions, is *Evolution and Revolution in the 20th Century* by James and Grace Lee Boggs. Written over forty years ago, it critiqued each major twentieth century revolution from the point of view that humanity is at a crossroads in terms of revolutionary approaches and they make the argument that the time has come for an approach that looks at the whole human being, not just at material needs. Whereas former revolutions were trying to 'get something,' the second American Revolution may actually entail giving up some things. **(10)** From this humanistic critique, they arrived at advanced theoretical positions on struggle that involve not only action, but also philosophically re-imagining the entire society. Many facets of this work are taking place in Detroit, Michigan. A school has been established based on their ideas on education and numerous community gardens have been planted through their Detroit Summer project. Learning of these various struggles allows one to see historical patterns as well as assess different strategies in the present day.

Another helpful book is **Movement of Movements** by Tom Mertes. Mertes enlists personal accounts on various modern-day struggles and creative approaches from the 'global south.' Whether it is fighting water privatization in South Africa, or land reform in Bolivia or the attempts at 'horizontalism' in Argentina to lessen hierarchy and class division, Mertes identifies several examples of fluid, non-centralized forms of struggle.

One example that has combined some aspects of traditional revolutionary struggle with the more egalitarian forms of today is the Zapatistas in Chiapas, Mexico. Sub-comandante Marcos, the Zapatista leader who has since stepped down, has articulated a far more inclusive ideology of struggle in a series of lectures titled, "**Them and Us**". (**11**) In these set of prose poem/letters, he draws lines of differentiation between the small numbers of people actually in power and their acquisitive, exclusive desire to sequester wealth and power regardless of the price the earth has to pay-and everyone else. This new paradigm draws a great deal from indigenous cultural concepts of egalitarianism, respect for the earth and its creatures, emphasis on spiritual connectedness, and cooperative political and economic systems.

Young activists with historical awareness might not feel so alone at times if they understood the struggles of those preceding them. Furthermore, if they understood that they were also part of a global movement that is building momentum daily they could feel more secure knowing they are actively participating to make a difference.

Be Proactive Politically

Find causes, big or small, that one can be consistent with and where small, periodic victories can be had. Choose issues that are doable and achievable, even as one incubates large visions of the future. This keeps one involved and continuously invigorated and revitalized. For example, if one is a health professional, administer free health or spinal screenings in communities where there is a need. This might include blood pressure, glucose, and cholesterol screenings. Getting involved in the fight against the oil sands fracking movement in Canada is an issue worth one's time as well. Cooperative housing to provide equitable shelter is an issue that is easy to rally around. Homelessness. Education. Hunger. Police Brutality and community violence. Anti-militarist demonstrations. By staying active in local issues, one can be more prepared to respond to national and global issues. In this way, the political activities are integrated into a lifestyle and can serve as social remedies to one's own problems. For example, working among people that are homeless can be, a good remedy for depression. In most cases, the people the activists are serving or working with have had a much harder time making ends meet and surviving than the activists have ever had. Working with them can often put the activists' problems in proper perspective.

Develop a Holistic Philosophy and Spiritual Practice

Political reality is just one version or aspect of reality. There is also nature. There is the vast spiritual realm of the unseen. There is indigenous shamanism where nature and the unseen come together. There are also emotional/psychological, gender, civilized versus non-civilized issues and paradigms as well. And of course, there is formal religion. A holistic worldview would have a compartment for all of these including science. Whereas one can only do one or two spiritual practices well, one's philosophy can be broad. With a broad holistic philosophy, one can understand that there is a spiritual component that undergirds life and it can possibly be approached and partly understood in various ways. The spiritual practice transforms the individual from the inside and allows him/her to experience the spiritual component for himself and be tethered to something universal and cosmic, less susceptible to constant change. Praying, meditating, singing, reciting, chanting, dhikr, dancing and ecstatic movement, affirming, even extreme exercise, all can serve as spiritual practices. In the context of political consciousness and activism, both the holistic philosophy, which recognizes outward and hidden forces, and spiritual practices, which anchor faith in direct experience and produces an inner light, are needed to turn the euphoria, anger, depression, anxiety, and fear into productive fuel for one's work.

Maintain Personal Relationships

Since the beginning of human evolution, relationships with each other have been key. Whether in hunting and gathering societies or modern day high-tech meeting rooms, the basic needs for humans to have positive interdependent interactions with each other has been 'wired,' so to speak, by the fact that the vast bulk of our time on earth, more than several hundred thousand years, has been spent in small family based units strung together by kinship and mutual needs. Not surprisingly, Positive Psychology now lists personal relationships as one of its components for happiness. Personal relationships, a sense of making a difference in the world, along with having basic needs met, are the main ingredients outside of genetics and heredity of happiness. (12)

Therefore, it is not surprising that activists who have strong interpersonal and intergenerational relationships, with family or others, appear more happy, and are often more healthy. They laugh more and laughter lowers stress hormones like cortisol. Furthermore, if one lives in a community, not only does one have his/her eyes and ears available to notice signs and symptoms of illness, one has everyone else's who may see things one cannot see oneself. This becomes more important as the activist gets older. Additionally, relationships encourage people to be more active because people use sophisticated and intricate body language while speaking face to face with each other. Interaction engenders movement. Movement engenders health and life.

A Healthy Diet

The importance of proper diet cannot be overstated. The old adage, 'you are what you eat,' is real. Yet, the issue of diet is controversial. Many activists over the years have changed their diets, particularly from a heavy meat-based diet to one with less or no meat, with many variations in between. Some activists have cut down on the amount they eat incorporating fasting into their regime as well. This prevents excessive weight gain as well as toxic buildup of wastes in the body. The idea in diet change is simple; eat the foods that provide the most nutrients, energy, and protein for the least amount of energy to digest with the least toxicity. **(13)** The most harmful item in the American diet today is sugar. Sugar, in its many forms, including high fructose corn syrup, sucrose, dextrose, 'natural sweeteners' and many others, over stimulates the pancreas to secrete insulin and its depletion causes diabetes. Sugar is also the main culprit in obesity and severely overweight individuals and combines with cholesterol in blood vessels causing plaque that can cause blood clots. Its elimination by itself would improve one's health greatly. Also harmful are genetically modified organisms or GMOs. More than ninety percent of the soybean and corn crops now have GMOs in them and their ingestion is causing 'leaky gut syndrome,' among other illnesses. These organisms have been ruled 'safe,' yet they are designed to make pests' stomachs explode upon being eaten and are increasingly being linked to a host of new, strange digestive symptoms and complaints including autism, infertility, allergies, birth defects, and even cancer. The only way to completely avoid GMOs is to eat organic vegetables, particularly soybeans and corn. **(14)**

But the issue of alternative diets remains controversial. Some activists have stated that vegetarian and vegan diets, for example, are elitist in that poor people often can not afford organic vegetables or shop at expensive health food stores. The vegetarians counter that a meat-based diet uses more carbon based fuels and water, pollutes the earth and vegetarians eat less thus making it more affordable. Lierre Keith adds a twist to the controversy in her work, **Vegetarian Myth**, by stating that vegetarians are also guilty of destroying the earth because of their dependence on agriculture. In her view, large-scale agriculture has shifted the entire focus to clearing off of huge swaths of land, which itself disrupts the environment, and pollutes the water supply with chemicals. (**15**) According to this view, even organic farming is disruptive. Those who advocate personal, raised plot, organic farming on very small family units or in collective backyards argue that their approach prevents large-scale agricultural destruction.

Regardless of these differing points of views, the idea that proper eating and supplementation is essential for health is being increasingly accepted. Also, more widely accepted is the idea of under eating or limiting one's caloric intake as a means of increasing one's life span, as well as increasing vitality.

A few other time-tested healthful tips include, using distilled water over tap water and eating at least 50% or more raw foods daily. Also, a good healthful practice is to eat foods with the highest water content first such as fruits, and any and all liquids either 30 minutes before or 3 hours after one's meals. In addition, chew food a minimum of twenty times before swallowing. Drink eight to twelve ounces of carrot juice a day unless diabetic, and take omega threes, turmeric, co enzyme q10, and wheatgrass juice. Fast on water or diluted carrot juice at least one a month, unless diabetic, and take a self-administered high enema with distilled water. More in depth study on diet and nutrition can be found in the classics by T. Colin Campbell, Max Warmbrand, Alvina Fulton, N.W. Walker, Rudy Ballantine, Paavo Airola, Max Gerson, RA Amen, Nana Kwaku Opare' and others.

A key concept of food and diet is eating according to one's activity. This means that if one is a professional athlete, one has to eat entirely different than an office worker. The protein needs and overall caloric intake would be different and attention would have to be paid to those details if maximum performance is to be achieved. This approach to diet is sensitive to body demands on a daily basis and one should fine tune the food intake with that in mind--always staying mindful of eating food that digests quickly and has little to no toxicity. If there is less stress on the system, in terms of toxic elements in the diet, the body is able to withstand more stress without negative effects on health.

Regular Exercise

As a reliever of stress as well as an overall boon to health, exercise is vital because it entails movement. Movement is essential for life. Exercise keeps the immune system working properly, blood pressure in check, and helps maintain lowered fat levels, preventing obesity and a host of problems associated with it. Exercise enables the mind to function better as increased oxygen levels help maintain alertness and ward off fatigue. The joints of the body function best when allowed to move properly and humans are 'wired' to walk and run very long distances without stopping. Ideally, walking/running should not be done on concrete. Humans have the most capacity to sweat of any creature and sweating has rejuvenating and cleansing affects. Indigenous cultures worldwide incorporate sweating sessions into their routines, which are passive forms of exercise, to spiritually as well as physically cleanse the body, mind, and soul of impurities and toxins of all kinds. Saunas inside modern gyms can serve a similar purpose. Even soaking in hot water is a form of passive exercise because the heat increases the heart rate while relaxing muscles and joints. The warm womb-like experience of being submerged in water is comforting and emotionally reassuring, which reduces stress.

Proper exercise also influences mood. Dopamine receptors in one's brain function better with exercise and dopamine is central to experiencing happiness. After twenty minutes or more of continuous exercise, the body produces its own cascade of powerful mood changing chemicals within the brain such as endorphins, enkephalins, endocannibinoids, and other endogenous opiate-like chemicals. These substances originally evolved to allow humans the pain free ability to walk vast distances and then track animals over days at a time. They prevent and or relieve depression-like symptoms too and could help with anxiety because they influence the part of the brain that controls feelings of happiness.

Other forms of exercise have added benefits as well. Both weight training and martial arts training are good in tackling fear because the personal power of physical strength, confidence, and self-defense capability carries over and translates into intellectual, emotional, and spiritual strength and confidence. Exercise also improves memory and prevents memory loss. Learning new exercise routines or maneuvers create new synapses in the brain and these new connections keep the brain active and vibrant. Exercise further gives increased and continued physical control and the feeling of being able to do things for oneself, even into advanced age, is empowering. Feeling empowered obliterates feelings of fear, anxiety, depression, anger, the stress of political consciousness.

Enjoying Nature

Experiencing nature firsthand calms an individual down because the body's master clock that controls the circadian rhythm, which in turn, controls sleep and many other unconscious functions, is reset. The rushing wind, running water, and cacophony of insect, bird, and animal sounds merge into a soothing symphony for the human nervous system. Slow, deep, abdominal breathing, while in nature, additionally adds vitality to an excursion in nature and makes one focus on the present moment. The increased oxygen intake invigorates the mind and body. Long walks in the woods, along a beach, or even in the desert, are relaxing because they tap into our innate, nomadic instinct and encourage contemplation. It is very natural to think about the intricate and symbiotic nature of the world and universe while in nature. The immensity of that juxtaposition puts the stress of politics and life into proper perspective. Life is more important than political struggle, yet without political struggle, one is not able to experience life to the fullest. Furthermore, in today's world, appreciating and experiencing nature constitutes a political act. Wilderness and old growth forests all over the world are disappearing and must be protected. But people will not fight to protect them if they have not experienced their wonder, majesty, and awe-inspiring beauty for themselves.

Chiropractic, Massage, Bodywork

Even though they are not as important as the things one can do for oneself, the services of professionals are, in many cases, helpful. Stressful emotions as well as events tend to store in 'muscle memory,' a physiological term used to describe the excess tone and firmness of muscle tissue as a result of the tightening, clinching, and shock of a traumatic event. **(16)** The event can be emotional, physical, or even imagined. The body's response is the same, to tighten, spasm, and in time, become knotted up in distinct areas of muscular tissue denoted by extreme tenderness on palpation. Over time, these areas can become very painful and cause spinal joints to become 'fixed,' or immobile. Chiropractic adjustments are very effective in restoring joint motion and once the muscles are signaled that the joints are moving properly, they relax and go back to their normal length and tone.

Massage work before and after an adjustment restores proper circulation and removes extra toxins that have built up in the tissue as a result of its function being disturbed by the traumatic event. Often, people will re-experience the trauma emotionally or at least be moved to reflect on it while receiving the bodywork, which has an energetic balancing and emotionally cleansing effect. It also relieves pain and removes stress.

Conclusion

Even though political consciousness and activity is stressful, not being politically conscious or active is even more stressful in the long run. The internal build up of seething tension and anger, coupled with the denial of white supremacy, racism, sexism, and capitalism on a conscious level, is a recipe for disaster. The psychic stress coupled with a bad diet and lack of exercise could result in a host of illnesses. Obviously, one does not have to espouse radical African American politics to be healthy or have effective avenues to deal with stress. But, if one is a member of the huge majority of people who daily experience discrimination and oppression, as most African American men and women, for any number of reasons and refuse to connect the dots as to why things are the way they are but have all the physical symptoms of stress and stress induced illnesses, their illusion is out of touch with reality. Life is stressful either way. At least being politically conscious and understanding what comes with it, an individual knows 'what they are signing up for.'

Additionally, understanding the stress that accompanies both political consciousness and participation helps one to manage what some might call 'contradictions.' Anyone who lives in a capitalist, market driven, technologically oriented, and scientifically and militarily obsessed nation, like the United States, and has some political consciousness while not buying into the culture of 'conspicuous consumption' and the idea of 'American Exceptionalism,' has to make decisions daily as to how much of that system they will participate in. To do political work long term, particularly while raising children, some financial and home stability is needed. Ironically, unless one is independently wealthy, the only way to have that measure of stability is through work that requires either training in a specific skill or a college education. The loans, usually from Wall Street institutions, incurred getting the training and education often demand working so-called stable, middle class jobs or professions inside institutions one claims to want to totally transform. For some, this might be considered an unresolvable contradiction. For others, they realize that nothing is perfect, and "actions are according to intentions." **(17)** Many realize that having the dexterity to participate in some parts of a dominant culture sufficiently to survive while holding fast to one's core principles and values

92

allows them to work efficiently long term and not get burned out.

Ultimately, it is about preventing cynicism and disillusionment. Understanding the stress of political consciousness could help prevent both because individuals would have a better sense of the multiple layers of adult responsibilities awaiting them and understand how those responsibilities could possibly wear them down. Hopefully, this knowledge could help one better manage and holistically integrate all aspects of his/her life while participating to his/her capacity. Sooner or later, everyone has to ask him or herself whether they have done as much as possible to make the planet a better, more just, more livable place and if they are willing to risk, sacrifice or give up something in this endeavor. Many who were active in the struggles forty, fifty, sixty or more years ago were willing to risk a great deal and did. It is due to their sacrifices that we are as far a long in our struggle as we are, despite the fact that we still have a long way to go. They had no roadmap to wholeness. In many ways, we do.

Presently and increasingly in the future, we will have to approach political consciousness and activism like a yogi. In yoga, all the physical postures known as hatha yoga have one purpose-- to strengthen the yogi's body and nervous system to withstand the shock of intense spiritual experience and endure up to eighteen hours a day of meditation. **(18)** Likewise, the politically conscious and active person needs to prepare their body and nervous system as well-by having group support, a clear philosophical and political vision, personal health practices, and techniques of inner development. In this way, people are physically, intellectually, emotionally, and spiritually prepared for the long haul.

Review Questions

1. Have you ever been stressed? How did it feel? Did you notice any physical changes in terms of heartbeat, perspiration, etc.? What happened if you were in a 'stressed out' state for a prolonged period of time?
2. Are people more stressed out today than in the past? Why or why not? What do you do to relieve your stress? Is it working? What else do you need to do?
3. Identify several historical figures that you admire that participated in the Civil Rights or Black Power/Liberation movements. Can you name some health practices and lifestyle factors that might have helped them relieve stress? Were there any organizational, workplace, or logistical aspects of 'struggle' that either increased or lessened their stress? Explain. How is their health at present, if living, and if not, what was the cause of death? Is longevity the ultimate measure of one's health? Explain.
4. Identify examples of individual stress spilling over and causing social problems in the community. How could these situations be avoided?

Classroom or Workshop Exercise #1

Identify a local elder activist that participated in the movement during the sixties. Rank and file members are preferred. In a short 30-60 minute videotaped (can use cell phone) interview, ask your interviewee several questions that you design. The

94

objective is to ascertain how their involvement in the movement affected and changed their subsequent life. Ask them about stress and how they have managed it. Have them state their name, age, hometown, organizational affiliation and occupation. Ask them their family status and how were they able to manage their political work with family life. (See "OG Says," an insightful elder interview project by journalist Pendarvis Harshaw for examples of how to respectfully interview an elder. Start by doing your homework.)

Group Project

Collect the interviews. Edit and put them all together for a short documentary. This works better in a classroom setting where students can collaborate with a video department. Use the editing systems available, either Premiere or Final Cut Pro. This interview project could be a part of the national project of recording aging Civil Rights activists being conducted at present This is similar to the 1930s Works Projects Administration or WPA project that interviewed former slaves, with some well over one hundred years old at the time.

Classroom or Workshop Exercise #2

Use the instructions on note taking in appendix 1. Read the chapter again, this time taking detailed notes. From your notes, devise a short ten-twenty question quiz, (essay, fill in the blank, multiple choice, matching). You will also use your notes to take your quiz. (Exchange quizzes, with you answering your neighbor's quiz.)

Be detailed in your note taking and individualize your notes such that they are easy for you to understand and decipher quickly. Design your quizzes to cover the main ideas in the chapter, with a slight emphasis on the solutions section.

Film Study

Also, view the film, "Happy." Even though this film does not address stress from political involvement, it looks at the intrinsic value of helping others, taking care of basic needs, and personal relationships. The film explores global definitions of happiness and shows that indigenous and grassroots cultures are often as or more happy than Western societies. Write a five-paragraph essay titled, "Three Things I Need- to Be Happy." (See appendix #2)

Somatic Exercise-Sitting Meditation

In Yoga, the breath is considered the link between 'conscious' and 'sub-conscious' activity-meaning that we breathe at night while sleep and we can concentrate on the breath consciously while awake. Therefore, it is viewed as the link to deeper levels of awareness and spiritual consciousness, resulting in numerous techniques on breath control.

Sit and close your eyes. Breathe deeply through your nose. Concentrate only on the sound/sensation of the breath going in and out of your nose. Focus all of your energy on simply listening to and feeling that sound/sensation at the tip of your nostrils. Continue for ten minutes. This is one of the first techniques in Vapasana Meditation from Zen Buddhism. Write down your observations.

Chapter 5

Prospectus for Manhood Training: Using Seven Year and Saturn Cycles with Emergence Theory as a Grid

Abstract

The universe, solar system, planets, and all natural phenomena function within and as a result of various cycles. These cycles interweave and interlock in intricate patterns creating big bangs, black holes, and supernovas in space. Additionally, they create weather patterns, seasons, storms and disasters, fish, animal and bird migration patterns, and all of life on earth. Humans experience cycles as well and knowledge of their importance could enable an African American man or woman the ability to simultaneously perceive and understand the meaning of an event on several levels. Furthermore, this insight could enhance growth and personal development while giving added meaning and depth.

Introduction

In his classic, *Cycles of Becoming: The Planetary Patterns of Growth*, philosopher and astrologer Alexander Ruperti postulated that each human being undergoes various changes and transformations that are conditioned by life cycles. These cycles, according to him, occur every 7 years and condition the quality of change and development during that period. The idea is that each 7-year period is governed by a particular numerical theme or focus and to achieve full development and

97

potential as a human being, understanding of each cycle's responsibility is vital. **(1)**

In addition to seven-year cycles, there are Saturn cycles that take place every twenty-nine and one half years within and surrounding the seven-year cycles. Saturn's transition, at least astrologically and metaphorically, represents major growth regarding responsibility in the individual life cycle. Knowledge of these life cycles, while not preventing occurrences from happening, at least may provide the individual a philosophical and spiritual context for understanding why an event is taking place. Additionally, their knowledge allows one to take some measure of responsibility for everything that happens in his/her life, even if in part. African American men's and women's ability to understand the significance of various cycles would enable them to more easily grasp the often-time deeper meaning and life lessons embedded in a particular experience. Certain lessons take place at certain times when one is at a certain age for a certain reason. Working with this type of knowledge requires a paradigm that places a high priority on intuition. The individual is able to glimpse the hidden world of spiritual energy and forces and yet, not blame the victim socially/politically for having 'bad karma.' The idea is to empower oneself completely, internally and externally, spiritually and politically, and recognize subtle patterns and rhythms while remaining rooted to the earth.

In the context of African American manhood development, knowledge of cycles and an attunement to some of the hidden forces of life, without overt religious references, could be helpful in allowing young men additional mechanisms to navigate society grounded in self-knowledge. Self-knowledge allows one to know more clearly what one can and cannot do. If one cannot do something, one is more able to learn how to do it, accept that one cannot do it, or find other means to achieve his goal and move on. A knowledge of life cycles, while not making one immune to stress, gives a larger metaphysical context to earthly experience that, when combined with earth and body wisdom and science, forms a holistic platform for looking at and understanding reality.

Ruperti's work allows us to see life as a process with various stages, each with their own theme. Even though there are many cycles, the seven-year span and Saturn cycles provide convenient metaphors to discuss growth and development. Just as there are increasingly more physical demands, as one goes from infancy to childhood to adulthood, there are increasingly different and sometimes more difficult life demands as one ages. Understanding the different themes or at least acknowledging subtle shifts that occur periodically can alert one to be more focused and vigilant in their personal quest for mastery.

Life Cycles and Emergence

One way to view these cycles is to ask the question, what kind of life lesson did I need to learn from a particular experience, event or situation? Or, why is this happening now (or keeps happening)? Life seems to be arranged and ordered such that we attract certain life experiences to teach us certain lessons. If the lesson is not learned, it appears as if the experience or similar ones keep occurring until it is learned or pivots into yet another more difficult lesson that still must be learned or mastered. It is as if we are all enrolled in a giant mystery school whether we know it or not or acknowledge it or not. Knowledge of seven year and Saturn cycles will not unravel these lessons or answer these questions with specific answers. Nor should they. But, being attuned to the differing themes and specific challenges of life at different times may equip an individual with the ability to envision several scenarios and enable them to make a decision based on those options. Furthermore, it could enhance their intuition such that in the future, they are able to anticipate the various changes that are about occur and have a smoother transition into the new cycle.

For example, since these cycles are influenced by wide variation due to biology, heredity, gender, race, tribe, sexual preference, ethnicity, class, nationality, geography, and other factors, the possibility for emergent phenomena as understood by complexity science is a possibility. The idea is that there are cycles, and within these cycles there are periodic upheavals or times when emergent phenomena arise that momentarily throws everything into chaos. Out of this chaos comes a moment of equilibrium until the entire process begins again. The universe is theorized to be similar in this regard. The Baum-Frampton model of the universe suggests an infinite series of big bangs and black hole singularities, resulting in successive waves of creation and destruction of the universe. Within these vast 28 billion year cycles, there are multitudes of unexpected, seemingly random events and explosions. **(2)** In his book, ***The Emergence of Everything: How the World became Complex***, Harold Morowitz describes emergence. Morowitz writes;

"This book on emergence deals with ways of thinking that are new under the sun: fresh perspectives for looking at the world that are accompanying the computer revolution, a new willingness of scientists to deal with complexity, and the very construct of

emergence that provides a clue as to how novelty can come to be in a very old universe." **(3)**

When the universe was born, created or re-created, it was an example of emergence. When the elements formed out of a "soup of nuclei," it was an example of emergence. When the solar system, planets, biosphere, protocells, one celled organisms, multicelled organisms on down to vertebrates, fish, amphibians, reptiles, mammals including apes and humans were formed, they were examples of emergence. Anytime there is a creation of something that appears greater and more complex than its parts, it is an example of emergence.

Looked at together, seven year, Saturn cycles and emergence theory may provide an experiential vehicle for aiding individual's ways to comprehend and navigate the immense complexity that life entails. ***How would this look in the context of an African American Intergenerational Men's group attempting to fashion a rites of passage and Manhood Training program for men of any age, but particularly for the ages of 14-28? And, how do we sensitize ourselves and our young men and women to understand that we exist in an intricately connected, ordered, and yet mysterious universe?***

Lets begin by outlining the various stages based on 7-year increments and articulate the large planetary factors along with the "soup of social and cultural nuclei" characterizing each phase. Then, what will follow are examples of life events or situations, based on life choices, which could emerge during that time. Ultimately, the aim is to try to fashion a workshop or series of workshops that show how using critical thinking, intuition, spiritual practices and concrete material conditions in the context of the above outlined grid can enhance and aid in personal development, particularly during the critical period between 14 and 28 years of age.

Overview of 7 year and Saturn cycles and Examples of events Producing Emergent Phenomena

0-7 years
Life Lesson: *Individuation*

This formative period is governed by the vibration of one and is about learning to be an individual. The focus is on the development of the self. Use of the word "I" a great deal. Often at the end of this stage, permanent teeth begin to arrive signaling the ability to take a larger 'bite' out of life, so to speak. **(4)** Emotional bonds are formed and a sense of trust established. The confidence gained in this initial bond of trust between child and caretakers or the lack thereof will shape the character and development for the remainder of one's life. The individual learns the use of their body and its various functions. The first inkling of personal power emerges with the newfound ability to walk, talk, dress, and go to the toilet, brush teeth, tie shoes, and write. First friendships, often with cousins, are formed.

Emergent Phenomena: IQ, wealth, birth defects, poverty, indigenous or westernized, rich or poor, person of color, white, mixed, accidents, good or bad schools, healthy, unhealthy, exposure to violence, etc. Much depends on parental guidance and stability at these ages. Children are emotionally and psychically attuned to the subtle vibrations and undercurrents within the home, good and bad. The child in turn, absorbs these, often unconsciously.

7-14 years
Life lesson: *Partnerships*

The number two governs this period and the youth begins to learn how to form partnerships: sharing, giving, and the give and take of forming friendships. Often at this time puberty happens for both boys and girls, as they begin the awkward phase of development when they may breakout with acne due to hormonal changes and so forth. They begin to develop the ability to have increased empathy and compassion for others. Huge growth changes with associated signs/symptoms such as joint pains, sore breasts, nocturnal emissions, facial hair, and growth in height are evident. The ability to understand the larger world increases and spiritual aspirations become evident. Social consciousness begins to develop.

Emergent Phenomena: More aware of social and current events, sense of accomplishment by graduating middle school, fear and/or excitement of starting high school, sexual feelings, 'crushes' on opposite (and or same) sex, physical development of strength, athletic ability demonstrated, aware of parental dysfunction, aware of society. Thoughts on their future predominate. More sophisticated beliefs regarding religion and spirituality, pro and con.

14-21 years
Life Lesson: *Group Formations*

Governed by the three vibration, there is increased social awareness and knowledge of the immediate environment. This period is the first leg of becoming an adult. The ability to function within a group is enhanced. It has many transitions and changes, including voice, facial hair for men, puberty, and continued growth spurt. Young people get a glimpse of how they will look as adults and the various categories they fall in. Due to the multitude of changes and outside variables, the years, 14-21 can be times of great insecurity and self-doubt. Boys become acutely aware of their height and weight and position in social hierarchies. They often seek out groups or gangs for camaraderie and protection. First sexual experiences often occur during this period.

The number three is represented by a triangle. It allows energy to flow easily from one angle to the next. Likewise, the challenge during this third seven-year cycle is to learn how to flow smoothly within the context of a group. For many, this is difficult and awkward period. Another challenge at this time is learning how to 'tailor' communication to a specific audience. For example, how one speaks to one's peers should be different than how one speaks at work or in class.

Emergent Phenomena: Street violence and school violence, clubs and school associations, outstanding high school athletic and or academic accomplishments, church or mosque affiliations, dating, gang formations, petty crime, family tragedies, grandparents may be ill or dying, may have lost many friends and one or both parents, aware of natural disasters, aware of global calamities, etc. If fortunate, this is a time of college and learning new skills and meeting new people. It can be a very exciting time. The flip side is that many African American youth during these ages attend funerals regularly and have a warped sense of time; twenty years of age is old to them. The multiple layers of personal, family, and societal dysfunction experienced at this age makes this group the most vulnerable of all.

21-28 years
Life Lesson: *Foundation for Adulthood*

The four vibration governs this period and four is the number of stability, the square foundation of life. It is during this period that young people begin to get adjusted to adult life. They seriously begin to think about their life's work and what it means to be a responsible adult. If fortunate, they are finishing college with a firm education to help them navigate society, or have attained marketable skills to find meaningful employment. If so, this period could be one of the most joyous periods of life. During this time, adventures, world travel, work within social/political movements, the starting of new exciting careers or businesses, are all possibilities. At this stage, some African American men are dealing with the aftereffects of poor education, juvenile delinquency, and petty offenses that have landed them in juvenile hall or jail. Many young men are dodging bullets from being in the streets all night with friends or gang members. The challenge is to appear to be 'strong' and 'represent the streets' while staying alive and, hopefully, progressing to mature thought and actions. Those that have successful careers can still get caught up in violent situations by just being out at night. Part of the four vibration is learning stability and this entails material sustenance and earning enough money to support oneself--not the easiest proposition in a competitive, capitalist world.

Emergent Phenomena: The full weight of society's dysfunction and unequal treatment of African American and Latino men are demonstrated by the incarceration levels of this age group. The less fortunate and less educated, the more physically threatening 'emergent phenomena' they will experience in the form of bullets, drugs, crime, sexually transmitted diseases, the lure of joining the army to avoid the streets, parental dysfunction, incarceration or death, death of grandparents and significant aunts and uncles, feelings of isolation, unpreparedness, and fear. The more fortunate, i.e., educated, industrious, skilled, and or independently wealthy young men, may experience some of the best moments of their lives as represented by college and graduate degrees, businesses, and international travel experiences. They may experience increased stress, pressure to succeed, and apathy. Fatherhood.

28-35 years
Life Lesson: "These Changes"- Adulthood and Maturity

The five vibration that signals change governs this period. The planetary lesson at this time is to understand that the changes that are about to take place internally and externally, are necessary and will allow one to take on more responsibility on all fronts. And, they represent a large significant cycle coinciding with the seven-year cycle. The large cycle is **Saturn.** Astrologically and astronomically, **Saturn** returns to its place at birth at approximately 29 and one half years. **(4)** This roughly corresponds to the ancient belief that real adulthood begins at age

30 and it is at that time one is asked to begin their real life's work. Purpose, meaning and an understanding of mortality all become more acute as the individual senses the 'speeding up of time' and begins to understand what life is all about. Unfortunately, many black men at age 30 are considered 'OG's' by then as so many younger African American men are dead before that time. Many have children. The parental responsibilities without adequate preparation and education create stresses that rob them of their youth and the need to survive sometimes leads to criminal behavior. Those not involved in crime, often form dependent relationships with women that additionally undermine their manhood, increasing anger and possible domestic violence. The big questions that Saturn is asking are, what is my real Life's work? What is my purpose? What do I need to do to accomplish what Saturn is asking? Saturn can be viewed as a portal through which to enter the rest of one's life. *It is essentially an opportunity gifted to the individual from the universe, but it demands active participation and change.*

This is where the seven-year cycle undergirded by the five vibration of change overlap because the five gives the individual the impetus to be able to make the changes that Saturn is asking them to make. Being attuned to the cycle beforehand would equip the young person with an impression of what the universe wants out of them, what it wants this person to realize about themselves, and what action to take. It is not the time to be passive. It is the time to do, and much of it will require some change. It represents the transition from young adulthood into full adulthood at 30 up to 35. After one has emerged from their Saturn return, approximately around age 31, one has a renewed sense of purpose. Often a newfound sense of power emerges that encompasses a more confident self. If the Saturn transition was successful, meaning that the individual was honest with themselves and accepted responsibility for his/her life and got clear on his/her purpose, the individual could have a feeling of 'coming into their own' with more clarity, vitality, and commitment.

Emergent Phenomena: If educated, technically trained, athletically lucky, or independently wealthy, this is one of the most exciting periods of life. Independence, youth, energy, connections, talent, and work ethic at this time lay a personal and professional foundation that can be relied upon for the remainder of life. Without these caveats and or privileges, increasing financial and societal responsibilities, possible incarceration, parental illness or death, debts, fast living, all could set the stage for serious personal challenges latter on.

Regardless of their place or role, the individual is acutely aware of the larger society by this time and their place in it. If there are feelings of powerlessness, they are often masked by individual bravado and machismo, which can exert itself in a variety of ways. There is the realization of being at one's physical maximum ability. One may have children to raise, feelings of inadequacy due to low position in society, or exhilarated by their burgeoning success.

35-42 years
Life Lesson: *Search for Harmony and Balance*

The six vibration that governs balance influences this phase. There is an acute awareness that life is 'no joke' and a realization that one is getting older. The search is also physiological because the metabolism changes around age 35 and slows down, partially accounting for middle age weight gain, joint stiffness, and degenerative health problems. It signals a major physical wake up call as the body begins to show signs of wear and tear depending on what one did earlier in life. Life begins to get a little cloudy with all the pressures and responsibilities of real adulthood. Yet, if one paid attention to Saturn and is fulfilling their life's work, there is an increased feeling of self-confidence. The individual is young, active, and happy and this could be one of the most productive periods of one's life.

If there are children, they are often teenagers and associated with this age group are all sorts of pressures the adult is now expected to have answers for others and be able to guide at least their own children to a safe adulthood. But, in some cases, men are still living with parents or off of women and cannot support themselves, let alone a family.

Emergent Phenomena: This is a time of accomplishment. The young adult has laid a foundation and could be in store for a promotion, new career or business, increased pay, managerial positions, and leadership. They also experience the full weight of personal and social problems. This marks the beginning of degenerating health and teeth. There could be prison records with felonies, many deaths of friends, parents and relatives, bills, unemployment, fulfilling career if trained properly, increased sense of personal power, financial success or failure, mental illness of self or loved ones, etc.

42-49 years
Life lesson: *Spiritual Search for Self*

This period of life is governed by the number, seven, which is considered a high spiritual vibration. Seven is the number of spiritual clarity and is referred to a great deal in esoteric literature, nature and folklore. There were originally seven planets, seven colors in the rainbow, seven notes in the musical scale and a host of other significant 'sevens.'

If one made it through the earlier cycles, one is very tired of flux, change and instability. It is at this time that even if one 'acted a fool' as a youth, they are grateful to be still alive and are approaching life very seriously. There is a feeling of "I hope it is not too late to get my life together and stop messing up." This feeling is there even for those who are successful, as well as those who are not. There is awareness, however, that life is not to be taken for granted and the universe has their attention. During this period, one is more aware of health, mental acuity and one's will power or lack of. There is an inkling that one must move more slowly, more deliberately, and more carefully. There is an awareness of the wrongs committed and often an attempt to make amends, if not too late. There is an overall feeling of 'wanting to get it together before age 50' that sets in.

There is sometimes a crisis at this time because the individual is half way through another Saturn cycle and at around age 42, it coincides with a Uranus cycle that can cause revolutionary upheavals. In short, Uranus represents Aquarian New Age values of bringing in an enlightened social order and distaste for the 'ordinary.' This combination with the 'conservative values' of Saturn can cause a temporary crisis known as the mid-life crisis. Others may experience it closer to age 50. The fundamental question that is being asked at this time is, "Did you do what Saturn was asking you to do back at age 30?" If the answer is yes, the individual just has to refine their agenda and proceed on with their life. But, if the individual ignored the lessons of Saturn or did not even glimpse they were being specifically challenged, they missed a tremendous opportunity for growth and advancement. Furthermore, they now have an emotional crisis, because the issues of Saturn that were never dealt with then are still there and the individual is roughly fourteen or more years older and has other challenges concomitant with the demands of that age. The problem is now compounded by the fact that what the person may have intuited as their life's work fourteen years prior is even more difficult to attain because the person may have to make more changes to accommodate their life dream. It is now much harder. Thus, it is at this age that many forego and give up on their dreams and never reach their full potential in life. That is why it is so crucial that African American men understand life cycles because many opportunities come only once, and if one misses them, they have missed chances to live with joy and enthusiasm in a career or life work that would have been fulfilling and meaningful.

Emergent Phenomena: If one has been working in an area of their life path and they have been fulfilled, this period could be filled with reaping some of the benefits of that success. There could be an increasing sense of mastery at work or career that is gratifying. There is a feeling of empowerment. However, there also could be an increasing acceptance of being middle aged, preparing for retirement, with emerging health and teeth issues, sexual dysfunction, loss and graying of hair, joint pain and arthritis, memory loss, feelings of being alone or feelings of being overburdened by family responsibilities. There may be a feeling of, 'There is no room for personal enjoyment,' or 'I can not in any shape or fashion do what I want to do.' There are often responsibilities to older parents, other relatives, dysfunctional siblings, adult children still at home, mentally ill children or relatives. There is increasing fear of street crime and vulnerability. This is the, *'You made your bed, now sleep in it'* - time of life. Whatever problems the individual has at this point, they can't blame anyone but themselves. And even if they do, no one cares about a near 50-year olds' problems.

49-56 years
Life Lesson: *Spiritual and Material Power*

The eight vibration of material power governs this cycle. The person wants clarity to see the outlines of the remainder of their life. Even though there are numerous degenerative and health issues, the person still has a sense of vitality and, if wise, really knows how to take care of themselves and what to avoid. They probably shy away from extreme vices, and are learning the path of moderation. The individual is in position to reap the benefits of their work in the previous years. Many world political and business leaders are in this age group. Fully mature, but young and vital enough to act powerfully. They are learning 'how to be old' and can see that their thoughts at this time are shaping and creating their life in the future. There is more interest in spiritual and philosophical and creative pursuits and if they have taken reasonably good care of themselves increased mental concentration and focus. There is a sense of urgency around personal endeavors because they know 'tomorrow is not guaranteed.' They are trying to achieve a balance between inner and outer life and approach each day with more gratitude.

Emergent Phenomena: Promotions at work, increased sense of personal power, ability to concentrate is greater, raising late set of teenagers, death of parents and older relatives, extra money, no money, debt, no debt, renewed focus, surgery, diagnosis of cancer, cancer survivor, memory loss, hearing loss, late divorce, late marriage, tax problems, early or forced retirement. Personal and financial success allows the individual to pursue more creative, adventurous, or spiritual activities. Financial ruin could necessitate starting over or reassessing values.

56-63 years
Life Lesson: *Universal Love and Appreciation*

The ninth seven year cycle brings a fuller vision of life and how interconnected all of its parts are. Nine is the number of completion and represents a comprehensive summation of life lessons. It is characterized by a deeper search for peace and knowledge of life. The second **Saturn Return** happens and causes deep introspection. Questions such as, how do I completely master my chosen field? Or, if I have, how do I effectively teach and pass on my skills? Did I make the right decisions in my life? I wonder what would have happened had I done _____?, what do I want to do with the rest of my life? Where else do I want to live? Am I prepared for real old age? Many other questions pop into one's head. The **Second Saturn Return**, which occurs approximately around fifty-nine years of age, marks the preparation to enter elder-hood fully aware of one's future responsibility to one's full spiritual unfoldment. There is often a subtle, but noticeable shift to desire inner peace, quiet, and a deeper spiritual realization. Yet, it is often a time of extreme personal crisis. The seemingly constant loss of mates, children, parents, friends, and others to illness, accidents, or violence, coupled with one's own personal illnesses or disability and financial stress, could make the individual feel as if they are bearing the full 'weight of the world.' It could feel as though the problems mount with a tremendous burden and suffering. For each individual, it is different, but the common theme with this or any **Saturn** cycle, is to experience some kind of personal upheaval or chaos that puts tremendous pressure on the individual to adapt and change in certain ways. If the individual is able to identify the particular challenge they are being confronted with and make the necessary changes, like being more responsible around their health or really listening more intently or whatever, they are often released into a personal realm of increased balance, clarity, and resolve. The person's strength is often renewed with appreciation and gratitude. One realizes that one has climbed up a major rung on the ladder of maturity. But, it is not easy. That is why an understanding of life cycles could help; their knowledge would at least alert one that 'there are rough waters ahead.'

Emergent Phenomena: Public accolades from a life of service, good health, world travel, second, third or fourth career, chronic illnesses, divorce, marriage, dental problems, feelings of personal power and accomplishment, feelings of bitterness and resentment, raising grandchildren due to dysfunctional children, insane or developmentally disabled grown children or grandchildren, illness, wealth, financial ruin through bad investments, poor overall health, fear of robberies and attacks, often preoccupied with bad news and world tragedies, deaths. This could be the happiest time of life if healthy and financially stable. The individual has a profound knowledge of their capabilities and has often 'mastered' some field of expertise or profession.

Advanced Age

As one enters their seventies, eighties, and beyond, the individual is usually retired and as an elder, is often in position to receive appreciation and respect from their community. Of course, this is if they were fortunate enough to have had a fulfilling job or career, good health, home, retirement package, savings, insurance, friends, and or a partner. If one is poor, old, and alone in America and totally dependent on government assistance or social security, without the aforementioned 'safety nets,' these years could be quite challenging in terms of basic survival. This is a time when, even in advanced age, one must use one's political and spiritual consciousness to one's own benefit by demanding one's rights and being vocal as regards their needs. Additionally, to the extent that they can, they must continue to organize on their own behalf and not allow themselves to become invisible. They must draw on an inner strength that has been cultivated through years of withstanding hardship and demand the highest quality of life attainable.

With the advent of nanotechnology/nanomedicine, improved holistic methods, artificial intelligence, and robotics, life expectancy is expected to rise to well over one hundred years. If that is the case, these cycles may be repeated in a single lifetime.

What that means is not clear, but what is clear is that people may have more time to make a difference in a significant way while finding spiritual peace and enlightenment. Either way, as one gets older, there is a certain amount of maturity and wisdom attained coupled with fear of death and the unknown. The person, if developed, can blossom into the elder statesman or wise elder in a council and be heard. In unfortunate circumstances, there is debilitation, illness and early loss of mental faculties. If lucky, most material concerns are secondary and the individual is freed mentally to pursue long lost activities and pursuits.

Emergent Phenomena: Feelings of peace, contentment, anger, resolve, fear, gratitude, joy, depression, and many others swirl in a loop either consciously generated or passively received. Many are still creative and intellectually and physically active well into their nineties and beyond. For others, it is a difficult time. Advanced old age involves more and more dependency on others and elders often are put in very humiliating and humbling situations. The challenge appears to be at this time of increasing frailty and disability, to maintain a sense of humor, grace and dignity and turn one's attention to prayer, meditation, chanting, contemplation, and communing with family, nature, and friends. But reading, writing, and solving problems are still very important areas of mental activity that must be maintained as long as possible. The individual often has accumulated a lot of knowledge that must be utilized in some way.

Many of the life lessons at this time involve accepting the help of others, if fortunate enough to have it. It is difficult for many because it involves releasing 'control,' looking at one's ego, and giving up power. If possible, one needs to be grateful and express gratitude as much as possible. Despite a preoccupation with self, the advanced elder benefits greatly by living in community, either with family, friends, or a suitable facility, as they are encouraged to interact and communicate.

Ultimately, one is preparing for death and how one dies sets an example for generations to come. The goal is to impart some valuable wisdom about the joy and privilege of having had a human life and leave one's family feeling renewed and strengthened by the courage and honesty one can muster as they face death. If one has found an inner peace by letting go of all grudges, expressing love and gratitude to all, and knowing within their heart that they 'gave it their all,' it is easier to let go. Of course, from a spiritual perspective, death is a transformation of energy and the light, spirit, vital essence, or élan vital, lives on and is either reincarnated, advances to other worlds, 'recycled' in some cosmic energetic soup, or dealt with in an infinite number of other ways.

Conclusion: How to Use this Grid

This is a rough outline of the various phases and possible emergent phenomena that can occur. A convenient metaphor to compare with the knowledge of life cycles is the understanding of weather forecasting. Oceans are alternatingly calm; mildy turbulent, choppy, stormy, or devastating like a tsunami. Knowing the weather forecast does not prevent the storm, but it does help people prepare safety measures by locking and securing everything and steering a steady course until it passes. This understanding essentially entails recognizing patterns. In many ways, life is very similar. Knowing the particular challenge of each cycle gives individuals ways to navigate through the various changes, hopefully having 'learned the necessary life lesson.'

How does one fashion a workshop or series of workshops that can facilitate someone learning to recognize life cycles and certain patterns? One way would be to devise a virtual reality simulation exercise that could project the young man through various stages of his potential life. He would be put in various situations, similar to airline pilots in flight simulators, and tested to recognize certain recurring or similar patterns based on hypothetical decisions throughout the simulated life. He then would be asked to utilize his knowledge of life cycles to assess the deeper meaning of each life experience and its significance to the life as a whole. An example is a tweaked version of the virtual reality game, *Second Life*, where people assume virtual identities and live a 'second life.'

A less technical and more somatic way is through role-playing. One can develop situations where one creates several factors that can produce various outcomes. Through role-playing, the participants can assume identities and engage in dialogue on the possible outcomes given the decisions one makes in certain scenarios. Then one can project those scenario's outcomes into the future using real examples, film, and street theatre. For example, for the 14-28 age groups, we can list a set of real life circumstances, such as a young man living at home with his mother.

To help embody the learning experience, the young man will be instructed to take on a 'role' and, with the help of outside volunteers, act out a series of skits that mimic real life experiences. The young man will then be asked to reflect on decisions that led to various scenarios and outcomes. One decision would be based on how they normally would have viewed the situation and the other utilizing their knowledge of life cycles. For example, one could stage a scenario where the young man is 15 and the mother is 34, having had him at 19. In this scenario, the mother has a college degree and decent job, but has early onset Multiple Sclerosis. The youth is smart but is 'acting up' and is now in continuation school. Does he continue down the path of non-productivity or does he become sensitive to his mother's plight and straighten out his life?

Knowledge of life cycles might help the young man understand that not only is his mother directly affected by her illness, but he is too. In his third seven year cycle at fifteen, he would have been taught that part of his challenge at this time is to become increasingly more sensitive to others and how to use the smooth flow of 'three energy' to balance out his activities and help his mother at the same time. He would additionally be taught that even though he and his mother are both affected and connected by her illness, they have different challenges. Hers is to grasp what her Saturn cycle brought to her attention a few years back around her life's work and to overcome obstacles and her illness enough to still do what she needs to do. His challenge is to stem normal teenage selfishness and self-preoccupation so he can realize that he is being called on to help his mother. His challenge is responsibility and balance--because he still must take care of his own needs--and at fifteen, he would be half way through his first Saturn cycle and astrologically and emotionally, being asked to 'grow up,' in terms of exhibiting more maturity.

This is simplistic, but it may be possible to devise a series of workshops and learning simulations that impart aspects of universal wisdom. They would allow a young person the ability to see that each scenario could have many complex outcomes and that they have *some* power and control over those outcomes. The goal is empowerment through critical thinking and intuition based on deep knowledge of life's cycles and the particular social, political and personal circumstances that could possibly emerge.

This is only a grid. Obviously, seven year and Saturn cycles and emergent phenomena involve much more that outlined here. Yet, with the above, one can begin to address some of the inner challenges of men and women of any age at any stage of their life without dogma. The central overall idea is that life is undergirded by a set of intersecting and overlapping fields, rhythms, vibrations, and energies that may have one source that, at times and under certain circumstances, can be understood. Understanding, however, does not prevent occurrences or guarantee self-mastery. But it will allow us to grapple with complex issues in a more intuitive, manageable way.

Review Questions

1. Have you noticed any patterns in your life? Any patterns in your parents' and grandparents' lives? Any overlapping patterns in terms of similarity of experiences?

2. What does the word 'cycle' mean to you? Is a spiral a form of cycle? What is the difference between a circle and a spiral? Are there any phrases or folk sayings that you are aware of that exhibit knowledge of life cycles? (i.e. *you reap what you sow*.') Who did you hear utter these sayings? Did you understand them when you heard them? How did the adults who uttered these sayings on life cycles teach the meaning of them to you?

3. What does the phrase, 'gut feeling,' mean to you? Why do they use the word "gut?" Are feelings actually located in the intestines, often called 'guts?' Are intuitions and gut feelings the same thing? How or how not?

4. Do you feel the future is preordained or is it being made daily by our thoughts that are projected forward?

5. How do indigenous people express their knowledge of life cycles? Discuss any similarities between how Africans and African Americans express their knowledge of life cycles? (e.g., John Kunering festival in antebellum America and modern day Kwanzaa based on harvest time, New Orleans style second line marching at funerals, Ring Shout, etc.)

6.   Based on your current age, what are some of the personal challenges you are faced with presently and how does your knowledge of life cycles help you understand their deeper meaning? If you feel they have no deeper meaning or significance, explain why you think they occur.

7.   What career path could you pursue that would allow you to help yourself, family, community, and planet at the same time? And, if there is to be more than one career, which is often the case, what underlying purpose do you see connecting the various careers or jobs you might have? How might an understanding of life cycles help in this search?

Classroom or Workshop Exercise: Film Study

View the film, "56 Up" by Michael Apted. This film documents the lives of fourteen children starting at age seven in Great Britain in 1964. They were selected across lines of class and gender, although there is only one Black child and four girls selected. It was filmed in seven-year increments based on the Jesuit motto, "Give me the child until he is seven and I will show you the man." The Jesuits, like many indigenous cultures, believe that laying down the proper foundation for a child is important and, if done properly, by age seven that child should have a firm sense of who they are, knowledge of their strengths, and an idea of what they really want to do in life. This film allows one to see how a youthful spirit with enthusiasm manifests in the ensuing years. Apted films them every seven years up to the last one -"56 Up"- that came out in 2012. "56 Up" allows a glimpse into the past and future of these individuals and it inspires the audience to reflect on their own life and how decisions have multiple layers of meaning and consequences that unfold over the course of a lifetime.

After viewing the film, write a five-paragraph essay titled, "Three Mistakes I Have Made and What I Learned." (See Appendix 2)

Somatic Exercise-Chanting

In a seated position, assume the upright posture of meditation as before. Concentrate on the heart area. In yoga, there are seven areas up and down the spine known as chakras. These chakras are energy centers corresponding to nerve plexi or centers. When one gets 'butterflies' in the stomach before speaking or gets a little nervous, it is the result of increased activity in the plexus of that region. Esoterically, the seven chakras and the seven vowel sounds correspond with each other. When that sound is made, the center is stimulated. The 'ah' sound corresponds to the heart chakra. When it is repeated over and over, it is said to 'open,' the heart chakra, thus allowing more love and compassion to enter the heart. That is why so many names of the creator have the 'ah' sound within their name. God, Allah, Yahweh, Krishna, Jah, Ra, Ahura Mazda, etc. For ten minutes, chant Allah, Allah, Allah, Allah, Allah silently. Then for another ten minutes, chant it out loud. Afterward, write down your observations. What do you feel? Where do you 'feel' it?

Chapter 6

Foundation Principle for Manhood Training:
Gratitude

Abstract

African American personal development entails having a holistic grasp of not only political and economic realities, but an inner philosophy and spiritual knowledge as well. Nothing is more fundamental to that than an understanding of Gratitude. As an introduction, this essay discusses Gratitude in the context of African American manhood and personal growth. It additionally outlines why gratitude is a foundation principle allowing others to easily flow from its application.

Introduction

In the course of devising a program and curriculum for training African American boys and adolescents to become responsible men, foundation principles are necessary. This is because principles contain within them virtues, values, and practices that have stood the test of time. These ideas have proven their efficacy and universality by providing humanity with core concepts that support and guide individuals through life's highs and lows. It is in this context that the first foundation principle, Gratitude, will be discussed.

Gratitude in one form or another is taught and embedded in every religion, philosophy, or indigenous belief system in the world. **(1)** There is virtually no language that does not have a word or expression saying, 'thanks.' Therefore, it is a universal practice. The English word Gratitude comes from the Latin *gratia*, which means Grace. **(2)** Grace is the often time prayed for but unearned reception of a blessing or gift. If one recognizes the numerous exhibitions of Grace, one can simultaneously be grateful to the larger source(s), forces, or processes that bestowed that Grace. Hence, Gratitude is both a philosophical virtue and spiritual practice at the same time.

This double helix type of usage makes Gratitude an ideal first principle because it is possible to show how other principles naturally evolve and flow from Gratitude alone. For example, Humility, Sincerity and Generosity all flow easily from Gratitude because by being grateful, one is acknowledging that there are powers, forces, or processes that are much greater than one's self and these same powers, forces, or processes have at times bestowed on one blessings and mercies that seemingly come out of no where. By admitting and recognizing that fact, one may be more able to tune into the connection between oneself and those larger entities, which by dimension and extension, demand Humility. And this Humility, earned either gently or through tragic events, aids one in understanding that while one is as worthy as anyone else on the planet, one is not the center of the universe and one is really only a spec on a planet that itself is only a tiny spec in the realm of all universes and creation. **(3)** Out of this position it is easier for one to be sincere, because one knows their place, so to speak, and is stripped of all pretense, arrogance, and excessive identification with the ego. Thus, one can be real and practice Sincerity. Likewise, by acknowledging and thanking the source of blessings, mercies and gifts one is strengthening their faith and sense of certainty that they, with proper attention and effort, will be provided for. If one knows they have abundance and are going to be taken care of always, they can be more generous and less selfish, hence, practicing Gratitude leads toward practicing Generosity.

Some may challenge the need for stressing principles at the beginning that do not manifest personal power and that as an oppressed people, power should be utmost in our consciousness. While acknowledging that empowerment is vital, strategic, and important, political power and knowledge without spiritual understanding and critical investigation of the spiritual source of that power does not adequately prepare one for the hardships and suffering of any life, even a materially successful one. Therefore, we begin with Gratitude.

What is Gratitude?

Gratitude is the deep feeling and conscious recognition of appreciation. Brother David Stendl-Rast believes it is the foundation for prayer and is often generated by surprise. In **Gratefulness, the Heart of Prayer**, he says,

"Our eyes are opened to that surprise character of the world around us the moment we wake up from taking things for granted. Rainbows have a way of waking us up. A complete stranger might pull your sleeve and point to the sky: 'Did you notice the rainbow?' Bored and boring adults become exited children; We might not even understand what it was that startled us when we saw that rainbow. What was it? Gratitousness burst in on us, the gratuitousness of all there is." **(4)**

Further, Brother David describes an instance growing up in Nazi occupied Austria during a bombing raid. While the bombs dropped, he sought refuge in a nearby church under a pew. He felt that at any instance the entire ceiling would cave in on him...but it didn't. He realized,

"My time had not yet come. ....I was alive. Surprise! The buildings I had seen less than an hour ago were now smoking mounds of rubble. But that there was anything at all struck me as an overwhelming surprise. My eyes fell on a few square feet of lawn in the midst of all this destruction. It was if a friend had offered me an emerald in the hollow of his hand. Never before or after have I seen grass so surprisingly green." **(5)**

In both of these selections Brother David is showing us that expressing and acknowledging Gratitude starts with simple observation and attentiveness. By tuning into surprise and not taking things for granted, one can be grateful throughout the day. Just the fact that one awakes each day and can see should make one feel grateful. Traditional and indigenous cultures throughout Africa and the world express this continuously by pouring libations, doing prayers and supplications for nearly every act or activity. Their stories, ceremonies and rituals all have embedded within them ways to express Gratitude.

Most African American people are monotheists, Christian, Muslim, Bahai', Rastafarian, Hebrew Israelite, Egyptian Maatists or various other syncretic forms of worship. Others may ascribe to Eastern Philosophies and Religions such as Hinduism, Buddhism or spiritual paths following the teachings of a particular teacher, Shaykh, or Guru. Still others have returned to

African or African derived religions such as Yoruba, Santeria, Voodoo, Macumba, Condomble, and New Orleans Voodoo. Regardless the religion, one can practice Gratitude because it runs through and is practiced in all faiths. Therefore, the teaching and transmission of ideas around Gratitude should not produce the enmity, violence, and dogmatism seen in religious discussions and debates. *Everyone can agree on Gratitude, even while disagreeing on who or what we are being grateful to.*

A Sufi Master of the tenth century, Abu'l-Qasim Al-Qushayri, wrote the **Sufi Book of Spiritual Ascent.** In the chapter on Thankfulness, he quotes the Holy Qur'an; *"If you are Grateful, I will give you more."* **(6)** Further on he says,

"The true meaning of shukr, thankfulness, according to the ones who know, is to acknowledge the benefactor's gift with humility...Thankfulness is subdivided into thanksgiving of the tongue, which is recognition of the blessing together with humility; thanksgiving of the body and limbs, which is characterized by loyalty and service; and thanksgiving of the heart, which is to withdraw oneself into contemplation of God's attributes with a continual preservation of reverence." **(7)**

As African Americans, we can also look at our history and struggle as sources of Gratitude. We can be grateful that our ancestors chose to endure the horrors of the Middle Passage and not jump over board. We can be grateful to our slave ancestors for having the ingenuity, cleverness, and fortitude to survive slavery and produce our great grand parents, grandparents and parents. We can be grateful to all of our great heroes and sheroes, known and unknown who struggled to help free us. We can be grateful to the unnamed, ordinary, brothers and sisters who labored to help build this country. We can be grateful to the Native American nations that gave us refuge and the European Americans who helped us through the Underground Railroad and marched and died with us. The list goes on and on, but the point is that there are multitudes of reasons to express and feel Gratitude.

The Practice of Gratitude

Contemplation of and cultivating Gratitude through philosophical reflection is very beneficial, but Gratitude's real practicality lies in the fact that it can be continuously practiced. Each tradition has time-honored methods on how to make the practice of Gratitude a daily observance. For example, Anthropologist Angeles Arrien, in her three part workshop and CD entitled, **"Gratitude: the Essential Practice for Happiness & Fulfillment,"** suggests writing down and reflecting on at least five things daily one is grateful for. This practice immediately tunes one into practical everyday things that should not be taken for granted. Additionally, it is an easy and practical method of teaching Gratitude to adolescents and children. **(8)**

Rituals that combine movement, drumming and chanting often make concepts like Gratitude more tangible, particularly to young children, because it anchors it in their bodies. In cultures where this is combined, as soon people hear a particular drumbeat or call to prayer they feel a shift in their inner state and feelings of reverence arise. Some African Americans and particularly Caribbean Africans participate in hours long Rastafarian Nyabhingi drumming ceremonies that give 'thanks and praises' all night long. The drumming and movement can

129

induce a trance like experience that embeds Gratitude into 'body memory.'

In the over 400 yearlong African American tradition, the Ring Shout is essentially a practice of 'giving thanks and praising God.' Praising God is a way of thanking God and that is an expression of Gratitude. Members of the Gullah community of the Georgia and South Carolina Sea Islands have preserved this practice to some extent. **(9) A community wide proliferation of the Ring Shout today might be worth considering, particularly in the context of African American Manhood Training programs.** Of course, the 'Shout' still lives today in its transformed incarnation as the Pentecostal Shout, or 'Getting Happy,' Holy Ghost type of possession. Even in this context, one is trying to express thanks and Gratitude by becoming 'one with the Holy Spirit' and allowing it to completely control one's body. This type of surrender is a form and practice of Gratitude.

In Buddhism, the practice of Mindfulness inculcates Gratitude. Buddhists try to keep their minds aware of that part of themselves that is permanent and infinitely pure by either meditating, chanting or counting beads while chanting. This increasingly produces Gratitude and Happiness because one is able to remain centered through highs and lows and one never loses connection and concentration.

Similarly, Sufi masters speak of Dhikr, or remembrance of God, as a way of practicing and developing Gratitude. Through chanting specific names of Allah, such as Ya Shakur, or thankfulness, increased feelings and understanding of Gratitude can result. **(10)** The repeated chanting with the proper intention gives the words more power to penetrate and reside in the practitioner's body. For this and increasing degrees of certainty and spiritual knowledge, the practitioner is additionally humbled and grateful.

The Benefits of Gratitude

The benefits of practicing Gratitude are immediate. As soon a one thinks of five things to be grateful for, they can feel an 'opening and softening' of the heart. It is as if the chest immediately expands and demands a deep breath. **(11)** There are probably untold reasons for this reflex, one being an immediate psychological check on how one may take things for granted. In that instance of remembering five things to be grateful for, one realizes that they, too, are blessed and have something to be thankful for.

Another immediate benefit of practicing Gratitude daily is that it can ward off and prevent much of what passes for as depression. As Angeles Arrien explains in her workshops, one cannot get rid of bad thoughts by thinking and concentrating on the bad thoughts. They are there and may have been there for years and may be there for years to come. She says all that one can do is replace them with good thoughts and if the mind and heart are full of good thoughts and feelings, there is no room for the bad. But, as soon as one stops nurturing the good thoughts, the bad ones will rush back in. **(12)** Therefore, it has to be practiced every day, preferably all day in some form or fashion.

A last example of the benefits of practicing Gratitude is that it prepares one to practice other virtues as mentioned earlier. By its capacity to lift individuals out of momentary despair, 'lack' consciousness, and fear, it engenders internal happiness. Even a small glimmer of gratitude, if acknowledged and expressed, generates a little light and soothes the heart.

Conclusion

In the context of African American manhood development, the practice and embodiment of Gratitude could change the arc of how young African American men are perceived within their communities and the larger society. By moving through the community with gratitude on their minds and hearts, their manners and outward attitude would undoubtedly change and with that, they would be received and viewed differently. ***This is dependent, of course, on their families, the community and the larger society doing their part to give these young men something visible and tangible to be grateful for.***

Gratitude is a virtue and practice that has a ripple effect. By taking time to be grateful, one is acknowledging a power or process greater than oneself. This leads the individual to notice subtler and subtler reasons to express gratitude until one is grateful for gratitude itself, grateful to be alive. When one practices continuous internal remembrance of Gratitude, their positive attitude and vibration attracts positive behavior and attitudes from others through the laws of reflection and attraction. Adults, like children, mimic behavior. In this way, African American men can re-write the stereotypical narrative of a crisis filled life with a story of gratitude, success, and overflowing generosity to the community and world.

Review Questions

1. Describe a situation where you felt gratitude? How did you show or express it? How did it feel 'inside?' Can you somatically/physically locate gratitude in the body? Does it reside in the mind? Heart? Abdomen?
2. Do you say 'Grace' at mealtimes? How does saying Grace at mealtime carry over to feeling grateful all day?
3. How do indigenous societies express their gratitude? What is a Libation? If you were to do a libation at a cultural event, what would you say?
4. Name five things that you are grateful for. Why are you grateful for these things or people?
5. How does gratitude lead to sincerity, generosity and humility?

Classroom Exercise-Film Study

View the Japanese film, "Departures." The film uses the sacred art of 'preparing the dead,' as a metaphor to sensitize the viewer to life. Discuss how the film relates to the discussion on gratitude. Explain how the concept of disgust can yield insights on beauty and creation and how the film's message of forgiveness can increase one's capacity for gratitude. Write a five-paragraph paper on "Three things I Am Grateful For." (See Appendix 2)

Somatic Exercise

List five body parts or systems that you are grateful for and why. Visualize your 'energy' or consciousness in those areas. 'Breath' into each area. How could this be helpful as regards health?

Afterward: Thanks

I would like to thank several individuals who helped guide and inspire my personal development. I mention them primarily because they did their work in obscurity out of devotion, commitment, and a sense of responsibility to their community. No one had to tell them to give back and serve.

Mrs. Edna Mays, who lived most of the entire 20th century in Pine Bluff, Arkansas, was an activist and social worker who, among her numerous accomplishments, helped found the Boys and Girls Club of Pine Bluff. She devoted her life to Civil Rights and the development of African American people. Beginning in the '30's, in addition to raising her children who went on to become Physicians and teachers, Mrs. Mays organized activities for neighborhood children for over fifty years. In the early '60's, she built a small stage and podium, with bleacher seats in her front yard for presentations, programs, and plays. She was keen to orchestrate situations where teacher's kids or children whose families with more resources played with and participated in activities with children that had less. If children were shy and unconfident, she would push them to the forefront and encourage them to speak up. She demanded total respect on all sides and forged friendships that still last. She was the first African American woman honored by the Arkansas State Legislature in 1973 for her work with underprivileged children.

At age seven in 1963, I along with as many as a dozen other little boys the same age or one year older, underwent a two-month long training and bible study class with our Minister, **Rev. T. D. Alexander.** We had a large church, St. John A.M.E., and for Rev. Alexander to devote two whole hours to us each Sunday morning at Sunday school made us feel quite special. The class was designed to prepare us for christening in the African Methodist Episcopal Church. While teaching specific bible lessons, Rev. Alexander took time to learn our names, our likes and dislikes, and what our future aspirations were. It was almost similar to that Jesuit saying mentioned earlier, *"Give me the child until seven, and I will show you the man."* This class was memorable for its closeness and for the fact that we discussed our spiritual feelings and thoughts publicly for the first time. In many ways, the core spiritual teachings learned there form the bedrock of who I am today.

When I was in the sixth grade, I attended George Washington Carver elementary in Pine Bluff. It was one of the best schools in the city for African American children. In 1966, **Mr. El Maurice Carlton** began teaching students how to play various instruments by starting with simple toy fluggle horns. By the time I arrived the following year, Mr. Carlton had organized a full, complete marching band comprised of fourth through sixth grade students. He individually taught each student how to play his or her instrument, whether it was the kettledrum, clarinet, trombone, oboe, tuba, saxophone, trumpet, or flute. There were majorettes, a drum major, and a dedicated drum line. He organized fundraisers to help some parents purchase instruments. I played alto saxophone and we performed all over Central Arkansas in parades, concerts, and recitals. Our band was the only elementary school band, black or white, in the state and maybe nation, all due to the incredible love, patience, and skill of Mr. Carlton.

Mr. H. O. Gray, in addition to being a minister, microbiologist, EEO administer of FDA cases, and Justice of the

Peace, spent many years as a Boy Scout leader. He was soft spoken and kindhearted, but was also firm and did not tolerate horseplay. Through our St. John chapter, he trained us in outdoor safety and survival, wilderness training, map reading, knot tying, and character development. I was a scout for two years while I was in the seventh and eighth grades. We went on long twenty-mile hikes and cooked over an open fire. We watched the lunar moon landing in the summer of '69 while on our annual camp on the Saline River. This experience gave me practical skills and personal discipline that I have used ever since.

My first martial arts instructor was **Mr. Clayron Rasberry**. He was a Vietnam veteran who had returned to Pine Bluff to become a Social Worker and began teaching Tae Kwando at the University of Arkansas at Pine Bluff. Several of his students were vets like him and he decided to open it up to teenagers and kids. I began studying with him in 1973, the summer before my senior year in High School. Although my intention was purely practical, as I wanted to learn how to fight better, I soon realized that the mental training, meditation, and discipline learned in Tae Kwando could be applied to all of my endeavors. The harder I trained; I became more focused at work and school. I liked the feeling of being able to walk away from violent situations with a feeling of confidence knowing I could have defended myself if I needed to. As a young African American man with no brothers or sisters, having that confidence was crucial. Rasberry was very patient, yet demanded total dedication to training and the proper execution of technique. He and Sonny, a fellow veteran and student shared war stories of real hand-to-hand combat. He did not take it easy on us because we were young or female. We did knuckle pushups on concrete, broke wooden boards, did demonstrations, and competed in statewide tournaments. I continued and received my Black Belt in Tae Kwando three years later from him in 1976. My training under Rasberry, who charged little to nothing, helped lay the mental foundation of my life in that it stressed discipline and self-control.

I mention these outstanding individuals, because we take for granted the everyday efforts of these kinds of people. They are the 'unsung' heroes that we have to recognize, honor and cherish. Communities are built and maintained by such people and we must create ways to institutionalize their qualities and teach those qualities to our children and grandchildren.

Acknowledgements

I would like to thank my family for their love, support, inspiration, critical feedback, and suggestions, Leonor, Chinyere', Xihuanel, Rukiya, and Jomoke. Additionally, Leonor's editing and design work is indispensible. I also thank my father, Joe, my Uncle Rosenwald, Twa, my cousin, and mother in law, Romelia, for their wisdom and love. Thanks to the Brotherhood of Elders Network (BOEN), Concerned Black Men of Oakland, the Office of African American Male Achievement in Oakland, the Office of Neighborhood Safety in Richmond, California, Alameda County Director Keith Carson and Chief of Staff Rodney Brooks, Lorraine Taylor, Cephus Johnson, Don Lacey, Pedro Noguera, Peter Harris, Cheo Tyehimba Taylor, Greg Hodge, Zef Amen, Ron Shaw, Howard Pinderhughes, Cedric Brown, and David Muhammad for the outstanding work they are doing for African American boys and men in the Bay Area and nationally.

A special shout out to Hal Clark of New Orleans' WYLD radio, Mtumishi St. Julien, Afriye Quamina, Pedro Noguera, and Tayari Kwa Salaam for their early support and comments and the Black Out Collective, #Black Lives Matter, and the Malcolm X Grassroots Organizing Committee for their outstanding work in the community.

Appendices

Appendix 1

On Note Taking

Note taking is a vital skill for high school, college, and work and beyond. It is the art of listening to a lecture, film, symposium, debate, colloquial or roundtable discussion, and being able to translate its most pertinent aspects into your own words.

Main Components:

1. Speed - You must be able to immediately understand the meaning of the speaker, presenter or text and write down in your own words, the main points or ideas, quickly. As quick as the presentation is made, you must be able to write.
2. Concentration - Your ability to concentrate solely on what is being said, presented, or written is important. Any outside distractions will reduce your speed and focus and subtle nuances and meanings can be lost.
3. Memory - The object is to always keep up with the speaker if it is a presentation, film, or lecture, but if and when you cannot, your memory is vital. You should hear the speaker or presenter in your mind and if you get behind, be able to recall, word for word, what was said or presented.
4. Comprehension - This is very important. If it is a difficult lecture, read materials or handouts before class such that the information presented is clearer at the time of the lecture. If

it is a film, read up on its contents by looking up a review such that the overall gist and direction of the film is understood beforehand. Use a dictionary for written material. The more preparation, the more comprehension.

5. Neatness & Legibility - The more legible and neat your handwriting is, the easier it is to study your notes. Also, the overall order of your page makes for easier comprehension of the material later.

Tips

1. Be Creative - Plain writing on a page can be boring, at the time of doing it and later reading it. Think of ways to make your notes interesting and come alive.

2. Use Different Colored Pens or Markers - One way to make your notes interesting is to use different colored writing instruments. Have near you, at least two or three different colored pens, a sharpened pencil, and a highlighter. Additionally, a little stack of post-its is handy for extra bits of information to draw your attention.

3. Use different Forms of Notation - Mix prose, short paragraphs, outlines, circles, asterisks, pointed lines, Venn diagrams, boxes, cubes, rectangles, pyramids, fingers pointing, artwork--anything that will make your notes come alive. Your notes should work for you; so let them speak to your individuality.

4. Be Thorough - Never be lazy while taking notes, they are your lifelines to the class. If the teacher is taking time to say or present this material, they think it is important. If the teacher thinks it is important, IT IS IMPORTANT and will be

asked later on a test and is expected to be understood when doing other assignments.

Final Note

Note taking is an art. As an art form, make your notes beautiful, creative and unique to you. You must understand how your mind works and in what format you need information to come to you for best comprehension and retention. No one else can ascertain that for you. Therefore, note taking is a form of self-knowledge, awareness, and understanding. It entails knowing how you are 'wired.' Some like more linear, straight lines, others circles, more others colors and symbols, etc. The challenge is to make each page stand out such that you can recall each item on your notes through memory, if necessary. Your mind is a wonderful 'computer' and part of this note taking process, as well as school in general, is programming that computer. You have some flexibility, but you must understand your own learning style. Note taking **is a first step in that process.**

The Twenty-Sentence Cookbook: A Simplified Look at the Basic Five-Paragraph Paper

The **five-paragraph paper** is the cornerstone of college level writing. Although brief, it allows enough depth to sufficiently introduce a subject, explain some of its most important characteristics, and offer at least one original idea. The easiest way to view it is mathematically. The paper consists of an introduction, body and conclusion. The **body has three paragraphs** for a total of five. There are **four sentences per paragraph** for a total of **twenty**. At the end of the introduction is the thesis that lists three supporting ideas that one will discuss. The successive three paragraphs explain the relevance of each idea. The conclusion ties the ideas together and hopefully suggests an original perspective that orients the reader to other ideas or references.

Title
(You must always have a title)

The Twenty-Sentence Cookbook
Introduction

1. The first sentence is the intro to the introduction and must immediately draw the reader in and let them know broadly what the paper is about by establishing a connection between you, your subject and the audience.

2. The second sentence expands on the first but begins to narrow the focus.
3. The third sentence offers a bit of freedom as long as it expounds on the subject. (no tangents)
4. The fourth sentence serves as a thesis sentence by listing **three specific ideas** that will be discussed in the paper. (this is the conclusion of the introduction)

Body Paragraph One
(Least important idea)

5. The fifth sentence introduces the first idea mentioned in the thesis and as before, must draw the reader in to the relevance of this point to the rest of the paper.
6. The sixth sentence expands on the fifth with important details, dates, or statistics.
7. The seventh sentence offers a little freedom to either expand on the previous details or introduce more. (add a reference)
8. The eighth sentence serves as the (mini) conclusion to the first paragraph and therefore must sum up, on a small scale; the ideas presented in paragraph one.

Body Paragraph Two
(Second most important idea)

9. The ninth sentence introduces the second idea mentioned in the thesis and as before, must draw the reader in to the relevance of this point to the rest of the paper.
10. The tenth sentence expands on the ninth and allows the writer some space to make sure there is continuity and flow

to the paper. (Other data could be used here, but be mindful of overload)(add a reference).

11. The eleventh sentence offers a bit of freedom as long as it highlights the second point.

12. The twelfth sentence, like the fourth and eighth, serves as a (mini) conclusion to the second paragraph by summing up all the points on the second idea.

Body Paragraph Three
(Most important idea)

13. The thirteenth sentence introduces the third and last idea mentioned in the thesis and like one, five and nine, must immediately draw the reader in to the relevance of this point to the rest of the paper.

14. The fourteenth sentence expands on the one before it with the most convincing data or information yet revealed. (add a reference)

15. The fifteenth sentence offers more convincing information as the writer begins to close the argument. (add a reference)

16. The sixteenth sentence concludes paragraph three (and in essence the paper) and must drive the point home to the reader with a logical and reasonable (brilliant even) summation statement.

Conclusion
(Closing argument, summation of ideas)

17. The seventeenth sentence is the introduction to the conclusion where the writer reminds the reader what was

said in the introduction and the three points mentioned and their relevance to the paper as a whole.

18. The eighteenth sentence attempts to convince the reader that their interpretation is relevant by possibly using a quote.
19. The nineteenth sentence drives the point home by explaining the quote in a new and fresh way and explains how it backs your position.
20. The conclusion of the conclusion should let the reader know what you, the writer really thinks. (An original idea or perspective that incorporates all that you have learned about your subject.)

This formula is meant only as a practical and philosophical grid. Or, put more simply, **Tell Them What You're Going to Tell Them** (Introduction and Thesis Statement), **Tell Them** (Supporting 3 paragraphs), then **Tell Them What You Told Them** (Conclusion). If necessary, the formula can be expanded to fit term papers, theses, dissertations or books. The key thing to remember is that a paper has form, rhythm, and cadence. If it has balance and symmetry in its form, its meaning is more easily conveyed and likewise understood.

References

Chapter 1

1. Lama, Dalai, recorded by Ron Whitehead, The Kentucky Center for the Arts, http://www.insomniacathon.org/nevergiveup.html, Louisville, KY., 1994.)
2. Madhubuti, Haki, *Tough Notes: A Healing Call for Creating Exceptional Black Men, Affirmations, Meditations, Readings and Strategies,* Third World Press, Chicago, 2002, Table of Contents.
3. **Madhubuti, Haki, *YellowBlack: The First Twenty-One Years of a Poet's Life, A Memoir,*** Third World Press, Chicago, 2005, p. XIV.
4. Starr, Terrell Jermaine, "Go Sista! HS Senior Goes From Homeless Shelter to Ivy League, May 28, 2012, News One, For Black America, http://newsone.com2017697/eboni-boykin-homeless-shelter-to-columbia-university/.
5. Shakur, Yusef, *The Window 2 My Soul: My Transformation From A Zone 8 Thug to a Father & Freedom Fighter,* Urban Guerilla, Detroit, 2008, Introduction.
6. http://en.m.wiktionary.org/wiki/f,http://i.word.com/idictionary/fortitude.
7. http://www.etymonline.com/ind...online.com/index.php?search=commitment.
8. http://www.etymonline.com/index.php?search=responsibility.

9. O'Flaherty, Brandon, Sethi, Rajiv, *"Homicide in Black and White,"* http//www.columbia.edurs328/homicide.pdf, 2010, abstract.

10. Nazim, Shaykh, **Mercy Oceans**, Book One, Shaykh Nazim Adil-Qubrisi, London, 1980. See also Shaykh Hisham Kabbani discussing Shaykh Nazin in *"Discipline and Spirituality,"* http://www.naqshbandi.org/TODO/sohbets/suhba/discipline.htm.

Chapter 2

1. Diamond, Jared, **The World Until Yesterday: What Can We Learn from Traditional Societies,** Viking, New York, 2012, pp. 1-33.)

2. Ibid. 1-33.

3. Gall, Timothy, *"the Aka,"* Worldmark Encyclopedia of Culture and Daily Life Vol. 1, Gale, Detroit, 1998,

4. Hewlett, Barry, **Intimate Fathers: The Nature and Context of Aka Pygmy Paternal Infant Care,** University of Michigan Press, Ann Arbor, 1992, p. 174.

5. Ibid. P. 174.

6. Diamond,

7. Ibid,

8. Hadley, Michael edited by, **The Spiritual Roots of Restorative Justice,** State University of New York Press, New York, 2001, p. 9.

9. Zehr, Howard, Toews, Barb, editors, **Critical Issues in Restorative Justice,** Monsey, New York, 2004,

11. RJOYoakland.org.

12. Stuckey, Sterling, *Slave Culture: Nationalist Theory and the Foundations Of Black America,* Oxford University press, London, 1987, p. 64.
13. Ibid, p. 64.
14. Ibid. p. 64.
15. Young, Jason, *Rituals of Resistance: African Atlantic Religion in the Kongo and the Lowcountry South in the Era of Slavery,* LSU Press, Baton Rouge, 2007.
16. Stuckey, p.64-75.
17. Goodman, Felicitas, *Ecstasy, Ritual, and Alternative Reality: Religion in a Pluralistic World*, University of Indiana Press, Bloomington, 1988.
18. Kabbani, Hisham Shaykh, *Nawari: Commentary on "Actions are According to Intentions,"* As-sunnah Foundation, Mountain View, 1996.
19. Vogt, Yngve, translated by Alan Louis Belardnelli, *"World's oldest ritual discovered. Worshipped the python 70,000 years ago,"* Apollon: Research Magazine, University of Ohio, Columbus, 2006, 2012.

Chapter 3

1. Boggs, James, The American Revolution: *Pages from a Negro Worker's Notebook*, Monthly Review Press, New York, 1963, See also *Who Needs the Negro* by Sidney Willhelm, *Future Shock,* Random House, New York, 1970 *and The Third Wave,* Bantam Books, New 1980, by Alvin Toffler, and ...*The Coming of Post-Industrial Society: A Venture in Social Forecasting, Basic Books, New York,* 1973 by Daniel Bell.

2. Boggs, Grace Lee, *The Next American Revolution: Sustainable Activism for the Twenty-First Century*, University of Michigan, Ann Arbor, 2011. See also *Living For Change: An Autobiography*, University of Minnesota Press, Minneapolis, 1998, and *Revolution and Evolution in the Twentieth Century*, with James Boggs, Monthly Review Press, New York, 1974, *Movement of Movements* by Tom Mertes.

3. Lynd, Staughton, *Accompanying: Pathways To Social Change*, PM Press, Oakland, 2012, p.1.

4. Ibid, P.1.

5. Goodwill, Alanaise, *"Leaders Walking Backwards: Male Ex-Gang Members Perspectives and Experiences,"* Kenny, Carolyn, Fraser, Tina Ngaroimata edited by, *Living Indigenous Leadership: Native Narratives on Building Strong Communities*, UBC Press, Vancouver, 2012, p. 229.

Chapter 4

1. Bloom, Joshua, Martin, Waldo, *Black Against Empire: The History of the Black Panther Party,* University of California Press, Berkeley, 2013.

2. Fanon, Franz, *Wretched of the Earth,* Grove Press, New York, 1963.

3. St. Julien, Mtumishi, Salaam, Kalamu, Ahidiana *Operating Principles*, Ahidiana, 1973, St. Julien, Mtumishi, *On the Shoulders of Giants: Ahidiana.*

4. Reynolds, David, *Morita Psycho-Therapy,* University of California Press, Berkeley, 1976.

5. American Oxford Dictionary, p. 81.

6. Barat, Frank, *"Progressive Struggles against Insidious Capitalist Individualism: Interview With Angela Davis,"* Profiles,profiles.jadaliyya.com/pages/index/19304/progressive-struggles-against-insidous-capilist-individualism, Sept, 2014.

7. Patterson, William edited by, ***We Charge Genocide: The Historic Petition to the United Nations for Relief From A Crime Of The United States Government Against The Negro People***, International Publishers, New York, Civil Rights Congress, New York. 1971, 1951.

8. **Robeson Testimony,** *http://historymatters.gmu/edu/d/6440/.* June 12, 1956.

9. Davis, Angela**, *The Meaning of Freedom: And Other Difficult Dialogues,*** City Lights Books, San Francisco, 2012.

10. Boggs, James, Boggs, Grace Lee, ***Evolution and Revolution in the 20th Century,*** Monthly Review Press, New York, 1974.

11. roarmag.org/2013/01/them-and-us-subcomandante-marcos

12. Harris, Peter, ***The Black Man of Happiness: in pursuit of my unalienable right,*** Black Man of Happiness Project, Los Angeles, 2014.

13. Campbell, T. Colin, Jacobson, Howard**, *Whole: Rethinking the Science of Nutrition,*** BenBella Books, Dallas, 2013**.

14. **Jeffery Smith,** "Genetic Roulette," DVD.

15. Keith, Lierre, ***The Vegetarian Myth: Food, Justice, and Sustainability***, PM Press, Oakland, 2009.

16. Chaitow, Leon, ***Soft Tissue Manipulation,*** Inner Traditions/Bear $ Co., Rochester, Vermont, 1980, 1987, 1988.

17. Kabbani, Hisham Shaykh, ***Nawari: Commentary on "Actions are According to Intentions,"*** As-sunnah Foundation, Mountain View, 1996.

18. Isherwood, Christopher, ***How To know God,*** Vedanta Press, Hollywood, 1953, 1981.

Chapter 5

1. Ruperti, Alexander, *Cycles of Becoming: The Planetary Patterns of Growth, Earthwalk School of Astrology Pub.,* New York 2005, originally 1979. Also see Dane Ruhdyar's *Rhythm of Wholeness, Saturn* by Liz Greene, and Numerology and The Divine Triangle by Faith Javane and Dusty Bunker.
2. Ghosh, Partha Pratim, Ray, Saibal, Usmani, A.A., Mukhopadhyay, *"Oscillatory Universe, dark energy and general relativity,"* Astrophysics and Space Science, June 2013, volume 345, Issue 2, pp. 367-371.
3. Harold Morowitz, *The Emergence of Everything: How the World became Complex*, Oxford University Press, Oxford, 2002, intro.
4. Khan, Inayat, *Education, Sufi Message to the West*, Omega Publications, New Lebanon, New York, 1936.
5. Greene, Liz, *Saturn: A New Look at an Old Devil,* Samuel Weiser Inc., York Beach, 1976. See also *Astrology: A Cosmic Science* by Isabel Hickey.

Chapter 6

1. Arrien, Angeles, **"gratitude: the essential practice for happiness & fulfillment**," Sounds True, Boulder, 2009, disk one.
2. Ibid. Disc one.
3. Personal Communication, Shaykh Yasir Chadly, 1994, Oakland.

4. Stendl-Rast, Brother David, *gratefulness, the heart of prayer: An Approach to Life in Fullness*, Paulist Press, New York, 1984, p. 9.

5. Ibid, p.10.

6. Al- Qushayri, Abu'l-Qasim, Harris, Rabia abridged translation by, Bakhtiar, Laleh edited by, *Sufi Book of Spiritual Ascent*, ABC International Group, Inc. Chicago, 1997, p. 121.

7. Ibid, p.122.

8. Arrien, three discs.

9. Rosenbaum, Art text and drawings by, Rosenbaum, Margo Newmark photographs by, *Shout Because You are Free: The African American Ring Shout Tradition in Coastal Georgia, Twenty-Five Songs as Sung by the McIntosh County Shouters*, University of Georgia Press, Athens, 1998, p.3.

10. Kabbani, Hisham Muhammad, *Rembrance of Allah and Praising the Prophet*, As-Sunna foundation of America, Mountain View, 1988.

11. Arrien.

12. Ibid. CD Three.

Bibliography

Books

Al- Qushayri, Abu'l-Qasim, Harris, Rabia abridged translation by, Bakhtiar, Laleh edited by, 1997, *Sufi Book of Spiritual Ascent*, ABC International Group, Inc. Chicago.

Angus, Ian, 2001, *Emergent Publics: An Essay on Social Movements and Democracy,* Arbeiter Ring Publishing, Winnipeg.

Arroyo, Steven, Astrology, 1975, *Psychology, and the Four Elements: An Energy Approach to Astrology 7 Its Use in the Counseling Arts*, CRCS Publications, Reno.

Bainbridge-Cohen, Bonnie, *Sensing, Feeling, Action: An Introduction to Body, Mind, Centering*, Center for Body, Mind Centering, Amherst/El Sobrante.

Bell, Daniel, 1973, *The Coming of Post-Industrial Society: A Venture in Social Forecasting*, Basic Books, New York.

Bloom, Joshua, Martin, Waldo, 2013, *Black Against Empire: The History of the Black Panther Party,* University of California Press, Berkeley.

Boggs, James, 1963, *The American Revolution: Pages from a Negro Worker's Notebook,* Monthly Review Press, New York.

Boggs, Grace Lee, 2011, *The Next American Revolution: Sustainable Activism for the Twenty-First Century*, University of Michigan, Ann Arbor.

1998, *Living For Change: An Autobiography*, University of Minnesota Press, Minneapolis.

1974, *Revolution and Evolution in the Twentieth Century*, with James Boggs, Monthly Review Press, New York.

Boyd, Herb, Al-Shabazz, Ilyasah edited by, 2014, *The Diary of Malcolm X: El-Hajj Malik El-Shabazz*, Third World Press, Chicago.

Campbell, T. Colin, Jacobson, Howard, 2013, *Whole: Rethinking the Science of Nutrition,* BenBella Books, Dallas.

Chaitow, Leon, 1980, 1987, 1988, *Soft Tissue Manipulation,* Inner Traditions/Bear $ Co., Rochester.

Cohen, Bonnie Bainbridge, 1997, *Sensing, Feeling and Action: The Experiential Anatomy of Body-Mind, Centering,* Center for Body-Mind, and Centering, Amhearst.

Davis, Angela, 2012, *The Meaning of Freedom: And Other Difficult Dialogues,* City Lights Books, San Francisco.

Diamond, Jared, 2012, *The World Until Yesterday: What Can We Learn from Traditional Societies,* Viking, New York.

Fanon, Franz, 1963, *Wretched of the Earth,* Grove Press, New York.

Ford, Clyde W., 1989, *Where Healing Waters Meet: Touching Mind & Emotion through the body*, Station Hill Press, New York.

Gall, Timothy edited by, 1998, *Worldmark Encyclopedia of Culture and Daily Life Vol.* 1, Gale, Detroit.

Goodman, Felicitas, 1988, *Ecstasy, Ritual, and Alternative Reality: Religion in a Pluralistic World*, University of Indiana Press, Bloomington.

Greene, Liz, 1976, *Saturn: A New Look at an Old Devil*, Samuel Weiser Inc., York Beach.

Greenwald, Glen, 2014, *No Place To Hide: Edward Snowden, the NSA, and the U.S. Surveillance State*; Metropolitan, New york.

Hari Das, Baba, 1970, *The Sayings of Baba Hari Das*, Lama Foundation, Santa Fe.

Hanna, Thomas, *Somatics: Reawakening the Mind's Control of Movement, Flexibility, and Health,* 1988, DeCapo Books, Cambridge.

Harris, Peter, 2014, *The Black Man of Happiness: in pursuit of my unalienable right,* Black Man of Happiness Project, Los Angeles.

Hadley, Michael edited by, 2001, *The Spiritual Roots of Restorative Justice,* State University of New York Press, New York, 2001.

Hewlett, Barry, 1992, *Intimate Fathers: The Nature and Context of Aka Pygmy Paternal Infant Care,* University of Michigan Press, Ann Arbor.

Hickey, Isabell, 1970, *Astrology: A Cosmic Science,* Altieri Press, Bridgeport.

Isherwood, Christopher, 1953, 1981, *How To know God,* Vedanta Press, Hollywood.

Javane, Faith, Bunker, Dusty, 1979, *Numerology and The Divine Triangle*, Para Research, Rockport.

Johnson, Don, *Bone, Breath, and Gesture: Practices of Embodiment*, 1995, North Atlantic Press, Berkeley.

Kabbani, Hisham Shaykh, 1996, *Nawari: Commentary on "Actions are According to Intentions,"* As-sunnah Foundation, Mountain View.
1998, *Rembrance of Allah and Praising the Prophet*, As-Sunna foundation of America, Mountain View.

Keleman, Stanley, 1975, *Your Body Speaks Its Mind,* Center Press, Berkeley.

Khan, Inayat, 1936, *Education, Sufi Message to the West*, Omega Publications, New Lebanon, New York.

1978, *Mastery Through Accomplishment: Developing Inner Strength for Life's Challenges, Omega Publications,* New Lebanon, New York.
1990, *Complete Works of Pir-O-Murshid Hazrat Inayat Khan: Original Texts: lectures on Sufism 1922 1: January-August Source Edition* edited by Shariff Graham, Nekbaht Stichting, The Hague,

Kieth, Lierre, 2009, *The Vegetarian Myth: Food, Justice, and Sustainability*, PM Press, Oakland.

Kolbert, Elizabeth, 2014, *The Sixth Extinction: An Unnatural History*, Henry Holt and Company, New York.

Lynd, Staughton, 2012, *Accompanying: Pathways To Social Change*, PM Press, Oakland.

Madhubuti, Haki, 1991, *Black Men: Obsolete, Single, Dangerous? The African American family in Transition, essays in Discovery, Solution, and Hope, Third World press, Chicago.*
2002, *Tough Notes: A Healing Call for Creating Exceptional Black Men, Affirmations, Meditations, Readings and Strategies,* Third World Press, Chicago.
2005, *YellowBlack: The First Twenty-One Years of a Poet's Life, A Memoir,* Third World Press, Chicago.

Marcos, Subcomandante Insurgente, 2004, !Ya Basta!: Ten Years of the Zapatista Uprising, Writings of Subcomandante Insurgente Marcos, AK Press, Oakland.

Marks, Tracy, 1985, *The Astrology of Self-Discovery*, CRCS Publications, Reno.

Mertes, Tom, 2004, *Movement of Movements: Is Another World Really Possible?*, Verso, London.

Harold Morowitz, 2002, *The Emergence of Everything: How the World became Complex*, Oxford University Press, Oxford.

Ngaroimata, Tina, 2012, edited by, *Living Indigenous Leadership: Native Narratives on Building Strong Communities*, UBC Press, Vancouver.

Nazim, Shaykh, 1980, *Mercy Oceans*, *Book One*, Shaykh Nazim Adil-Qubrisi, London.
2002, Liberating The Soul Vol. 1-2, Islamic Supreme Council of America, Washington D.C.

Noguera, Pedro, 2008, *The Trouble With Black Boys: And Other Reflections on Race, Equity, and the Future of Education*, Jossey-Bass, San Francisco.
Noguera, Pedro, Hurtado, Aida, Fergus, Edward, 2012, *Invisible No More: Understanding the Disenfranchisement of Latino Boys* and Men, Routledge, New York.

Patterson, William edited by, 1952, 1971, *We Charge Genocide*: *The Historic Petition to the United Nations for Relief From A Crime Of The United States Government Against The Negro People*, International Publishers, New York, Civil Rights Congress, New York.

Peters, Erskine, 1986, *African Openings To The Tree of Life*, The Warren Press, Oakland.

Reynolds, David, 1976, *Morita Psycho-Therapy,* University of California Press, Berkeley.

Rosenbaum, Art text and drawings by, Rosenbaum, Margo Newmark photographs by, 1998, *Shout Because You are Free: The African American Ring Shout Tradition in Coastal Georgia, Twenty-Five Songs as Sung by the McIntosh County Shouters*, University of Georgia Press, Athens.

Rudhyar, Dane, 1983, *Rhythm of Wholeness*, Theosophical Publishing House, Wheaton.

Ruperti, Alexander, 1979, 2005, *Cycles of Becoming: The Planetary Patterns of Growth*, Earthwalk School of Astrology Pub., New York.

Sardar, Ziaudin, Abrams, Iwona, 2008, *Introducing Chaos: A Graphic Guide,* Icon, Cambridge.

Shakur, Yusef, 2008, *The Window 2 My Soul: My Transformation From A Zone 8 Thug to a Father & Freedom Fighter,* Urban Guerilla, Detroit.

Solnit, Rebecca, 2009, *A Paradise Built in Hell: The Extraordinary Communities That Arise in Disasters*, Penguin, New York.

Stendl-Rast, Brother David, 1984, *gratefulness, the heart of prayer: An Approach to Life in Fullness*, Paulist Press, New York.

St. Julien, Mtumishi, Salaam, Kalamu, Ahidiana 1973, *Operating Principles*, Ahidiana.

Strang, Heather, Braithwaite, John edited by, 2001, *Restorative Justice and Civil Society*, Cambridge University Press, Cambridge.

Stuckey, Sterling, 1987, *Slave Culture: Nationalist Theory and the Foundations Of Black America*, Oxford University press, London.

Toffler, Alvin, *1970*, *Future Shock*, **Random House, New York,** 1980, *The Third Wave*, Bantam Books, New York.

Tutashinda, K., 1985, 2015, *Toward a Holistic Worldview: Essays on Control, Technology, & Personal/Social Transformation,* Imhotep Publishing, Berkeley.
2013, *Whose Future Is It? Social Control and the Health of African American Boys and Men*, Imhotep Publishing, Berkeley.
2014, *Political Consciousness as a Prerequisite Vol. 1.: On African American Manhood, Race, and Legal History*, Imhotep Publishing, Berkeley.

West, Cornel edited by, 1997, *Restoring Hope: Conversations on the Future of Black America, Beacon Press, Boston.*

Willhelm, Sidney, 1970, *Who Needs The Negro,* Bantum Books, New York.

Yogananda, Paramhamsa, 1946, *Autobiography of a Yogi*, Self-Realization Fellowship, Pacific Palisades.

Young, Jason, 2007, *Rituals of Resistance: African Atlantic Religion in the Kongo and the Lowcountry South in the Era of Slavery,* Louisiana State University Press, Baton Rouge.

Vivekananda, Swami, 1953, *The Four Yogas and Other Works*, Vedanta Society of St. Louis,

Zehr, Howard, Toews, Barb, editors, 2004, *Critical Issues in Restorative Justice,* Monsey, New York.

Articles

Barat, Frank, *"Progressive Struggles against Insidous Capitalist Individualism: Interview With Angela Davis,"* Profiles,profiles.jadaliyya.com/pages/index/19304/progressive-struggles-against-insidous-capilist-individualism, Sept, 2014.

Goodwill, Alanaise, *"Leaders Walking Backwards: Male Ex-Gang Members Perspectives and Experiences,"* Kenny, Carolyn, Fraser, Tina Ngaroimata edited by, *Living Indigenous Leadership: Native Narratives on Building Strong Communities*, UBC Press, Vancouver, 2012.

Kabbani, Hisham Shaykh, *"Discipline and Spirituality,"* http://www.naqshbandi.org/TODO/sohbets/suhba/discipline.

Lama, Dalai, recorded by Ron Whitehead, The Kentucky Center for the Arts, http://www.insomniacathon.org/nevergiveup.html, Louisville, KY., 1994.

Marcos, roarmag.org/2013/01/them-and-us-subcomandante-marcos.

O'Flaherty, Brandon, Sethi, Rajiv, *"Homicide in Black and White,"* http//www.columbia.edurs328/homicide.pdf, 2010.

Robeson Testimony, *http://historymatters.gmu/edu/d/6440/.* June 12, 1956.

Starr, Terrell Jermaine, "Go Sista! HS Senior Goes From Homeless Shelter to Ivy League, May 28, 2012, News One, For Black America, http://newsone.com2017697/eboni-boykin-homeless-shelter-to-columbia-university/.

Vogt, Yngve, translated by Alan Loius Belardnelli, *"World's oldest ritual discovered. Worshipped the python 70,000 years ago,"* Apollon: Research Magazine, University of Ohio, Columbus, 2006, 2012.

About the Author

K. Tutashinda, D.C. (Brian Porche' Altheimer), is a Chiropractor, teacher, activist/consultant, and independent scholar. He has been in private practice since 1989 and owns Imhotep Chiropractic & Wellness Center in Berkeley, California. He teaches English in the Upward Bound Program at Mills College in Oakland, California and taught and led workshops in UC Berkeley's program for twenty-eight years, beginning in 1984. He has also taught in the Oakland Unified School District, at Life Chiropractic College West, JFK University, and New College of California.

He teaches and leads workshops through his consulting service, Nano Education Project, on the benefits and potential hazards of nanotechnology and other emergent technologies. The author of eight books, he graduated with a Bachelor of Arts degree in Philosophy from the University of Arkansas at Fayetteville and a Doctor of Chiropractic degree from Life Chiropractic College West. He is married with four adult children and lives in the Bay Area, Northern California.

www.ingramcontent.com/pod-product-compliance
Lightning Source LLC
Chambersburg PA
CBHW061045110426
42740CB00049B/2186